code+2/0305

HERTFORDSHIRE WALKS FO

Warne Gerrard Guides for Walkers

Walks for Motorists Series

CHESHIRE WALKS
CHILTERNS WALKS
        Northern
        Southern
COTSWOLD WALKS
        Northern
        Southern
COUNTY OF AVON WALKS
COUNTY OF DURHAM WALKS
DARTMOOR WALKS
DERBYSHIRE WALKS
        Northern
        Southern
DORSET WALKS
ESSEX WALKS
EXMOOR WALKS
FAMILY WALKS IN MIDLAND COUNTIES
FURTHER CHESHIRE WALKS
FURTHER DALES WALKS
GREEN LONDON WALKS (both circular and cross country)
HAMPSHIRE AND THE NEW FOREST WALKS
HERTFORDSHIRE WALKS
ISLE OF WIGHT WALKS
JERSEY WALKS
KENT WALKS
LAKE DISTRICT WALKS
        Central
        Northern
        Western
LOTHIAN AND SOUTH EAST BORDERS WALKS
MIDLAND WALKS
NORTHUMBERLAND WALKS
NORTH YORK MOORS WALKS
        North and East
        West and South
PEAK DISTRICT WALKS
PENDLESIDE AND BRONTE COUNTRY WALKS
SEVERN VALLEY WALKS
SNOWDONIA WALKS Northern
SOUTH DEVON WALKS
SOUTH DOWNS WALKS
SURREY WALKS
WYE VALLEY WALKS
YORKSHIRE DALES WALKS

Long Distance and Cross Country Walks

RAMBLES IN THE DALES
WALKING THE PENNINE WAY

HERTFORDSHIRE

WALKS FOR MOTORISTS

Wm. A. Bagley

**30 circular walks
with sketch maps by
the author**

FREDERICK WARNE

Published by
Frederick Warne (Publishers) Ltd
40 Bedford Square
London WC1B 3HE

© Wm. A. Bagley 1975, 1982

Walks 1—23 first published in *London Countryside Walks for Motorists: North Western Area*, 1975; Walks 25—29 first published in *London Countryside Walks for Motorists: North Eastern Area*, 1977

First published in this edition 1982

Publishers' Note

While every care has been taken in the compilation of this book, the publishers cannot accept responsibility for any inaccuracies. But things may have changed since the book was published: paths are sometimes diverted, a concrete bridge may replace a wooden one, stiles disappear. Please let the publishers know if you discover anything like this on your way.

The length of each walk in this book is given in miles and kilometres, but within the text imperial measurements are quoted. It is useful to bear the following approximations in mind: 5 miles = 8 kilometres, ½ mile = 800 metres, 1 metre = 39 inches.

ISBN 0 7232 2809 4

Printed by Galava Printing Company Limited, Nelson, Lancashire

Contents

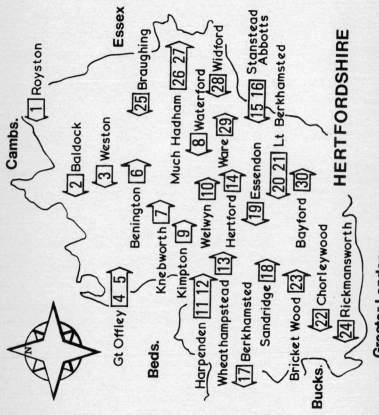

Cambs.

Essex

Royston 1

Baldock 2

Weston 3

Benington 6

Braughing 25

Much Hadham 26 27

Waterford 28

Widford

Knebworth 7

Welwyn 10

Hertford 14

Ware 29

Essendon 19

20 21 Lt Berkhamsted

Stanstead Abbotts 15 16

Bayford 30

Gt Offley 4 5

Kimpton 9

Harpenden 11 12

Wheathampstead 13

Sandridge 18

Chorleywood 22

Rickmansworth 24

Bricket Wood 23

Berkhamsted 17

Beds.

Bucks.

Greater London

HERTFORDSHIRE

N

Introduction

This book is concentrated on walks in Hertfordshire, with, in one case (Walk 24) a brief overspill into the London Borough of Hillingdon for the purpose of seeing an interesting boundary mark. Its genesis was in two previous books: *London Countryside Walks for Motorists: North Western Area,* which took in some walks in Buckinghamshire, and *London Countryside Walks for Motorists: North Eastern Area.* Whilst the majority of the rambles in this latter book were in Essex some were in Hertfordshire.

Since there seems to be a decided preference for walks to be classified by *county,* I have gathered the Hertfordshire rambles into this present volume. In so doing I have taken the opportunity of some updating and have avoided areas where new road works are likely, in the near future, to disrupt the old pattern of footpaths; that is, as far as the intentions of the Hertfordshire County Council and the Ministry of Transport have been revealed. There is always talk of new bypasses—at Baldock, Watton, Berkhamsted, Redbourn and at Stanstead Abbotts, for example—but if these materialize they will probably not come within the life-span of the present edition of walks. Road numbering can change, too.

All the walks have been tried out, most of them many times over the years, and only those paths and bridleways reasonably likely to remain walkable have been used. I have often been accused by footpath 'hearties' of describing only the generally 'easy' paths, making them more and more used, whilst the 'difficult' paths (the ploughed-up ones over vast rough fields and the somewhat overgrown bridleways, for example) become less and less used and farmers and landowners are encouraged to give such ancient rights of way a quietus, illegally.

I sincerely hope that if the walks in this present book have encouraged an interest in country walking, by providing mostly trouble-free routes (though there are a few places where you may literally have to take the rough with the smooth), the reader may, especially by joining a local footpath society or by individual effort, help to 'show the flag' over the more obscure paths. Membership of the Ramblers' Association (1/5 Wandsworth Road, London SW8 2LJ) and study of their footpath policy publications is highly recommended.

Whilst immediate major changes on my routes are not anticipated some minor ones may be encountered. It may happen that a change of weather may compel an alternative route or the shades of night may be falling fast. For this reason many walkers like to carry an Ordnance Survey map, which in any case gives more 'background' detail than the simple sketch maps can. The number of the relevant OS map on the 1:50,000 scale (2 cm to 1 km, or roughly 1¼ in to the mile) is given at the head of each walk.

So far as is humanly possible to check from current definitive maps and by actual survey, all the paths described are believed to be public rights of way (with the exception of a very few noted as 'probably permissive'). Please keep strictly to the line of path, bearing in mind that what is recreational to you is livelihood to the farmer.

If snags are encountered I would be grateful if you would inform me c/o the publisher. It cannot be too strongly emphasized, however, that if at any time you find that the description in the book does not tally with your present position, it is far better (and usually saves time in the end) to *go back to the last 'sure' point and try again*. It may well be that a trick of the lighting or of foliage has misled you, or that some other beguiling path has enticed you. Never attempt to retrieve your position by taking unauthorized short cuts over private land.

If you give every word of my description its due weight and are prepared to make occasional slight adjustments to cope with the inevitable changes in farming and estate management patterns, your walks in 'Hearty, homely, loving Hertfordshire'—a small county still with a great deal of rural charm and within easy reach by car of the Metropolis—should be very enjoyable. It only remains for me to wish you happy walking and fine weather.

The following will help you to interpret the sketch maps:

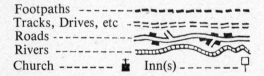

The inn symbol merely indicates that there is at least one inn in the town or village named. In the text the inns are named as locating points on the route.

I have refrained from indicating opening times of historic houses and the like open to the public, since details can change from one season to another. In the reference section of most public libraries, however, one can consult the National Trust's current handbook for lists of houses and gardens open to the public.

Acknowledgements

I am greatly indebted to my brother John and to my good companions of the footpath way, A. Geoffrey Stevenson and Colin H. Hills, not only for re-walking and checking, between them, many of the ramble routes in this edition and in the original edition, but also for their constructive criticism and valuable advice. If, despite this vetting, any minor slips have crept in, well—seeking refuge behind a Latin tag—*mea culpa*.

Walk 1

**Royston, Therfield
and Reed**

9 miles (14.5 km)

OS sheet 166

Royston is on the A10, 41 miles north of London. Park in the main car park in Barkway Street, opposite the Green Man.

Royston, which is Hertfordshire's most northerly town, close to the Cambridgeshire border, makes a good base for a whole day walk and, moreover, has much of interest in itself. There is, for example, the famous Royston Cave in Melbourne Street near the latter's junction with Kneesworth Street, where are ancient chalk carvings of St Christopher, St Catherine and many more. It would be a good idea to check times of opening when you first arrive in the town so as to decide whether to make the visit before or after your walk. The church, a short way up Melbourne Street, has interesting possessions: something, I think, from every century since it was built.

On your outward way you will notice, on the skyline at Therfield Heath, some tumuli (ancient burial mounds). If you have time and energy after the main walk they are worth visiting, if only for the good views.

The walk begins at the main car park above mentioned. Turn left and then cross the London Road to go up Sun Hill opposite. Where this meets the transverse Briary Lane turn left along a rising track, soon passing Heath Farm (formerly, as older maps show, named Wicker Hall). Later you pass a reservoir compound on your left.

Later with fine views ahead bend squarely rightwards with the clear, wide, grassy track and subsequently bend squarely leftwards with it. A pleasant line of trees stretches ahead and you are now on a fine bridleway. Keep absolutely straight on. Later, after a rising section, you come to a kind of small triangular green (point X).

I will assume that (at about 3 miles from your starting point) you will wish to detour to the inn at Therfield — though the walk will, of course, be a little shorter if you don't! For the detour turn rightwards, the track becoming a rough lane which joins a transverse road (The Causeway) in which you turn left soon to reach the Fox and Duck at Therfield.

Return to point X. Here the way is leftwards from your original approach from Royston.

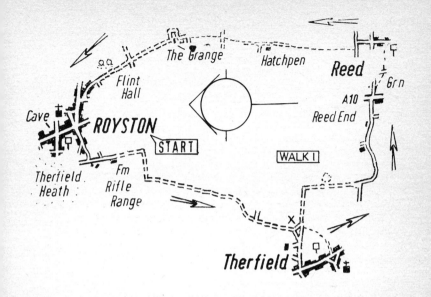

Keep forward on a track at first hedged on both sides but soon open on one. Follow this clear track for a short ½ mile. Then turn squarely right, soon passing on your left a conspicuous tree-girdled old chalk pit which you will have noticed from afar.

Keep absolutely straight on. Later a cottage ahead marks a road but just before reaching it, veer half right. In the lane turn leftwards and soon fork leftwards. Follow out, past Reed End to the main road (the A10) at the Silver Ball restaurant and garage. Turn rightwards for a few yards and then leftwards (for Reed).

On reaching Reed village green go diagonally across it to the far right-hand corner and across the lane and get over a field gate. Cross a meadow to a similar gate (the theoretical line of the path may possibly go through one of the adjacent hedge gaps). Then bear just a merest trifle rightwards, passing a little pond on your right, to climb over wooden bars near the right-hand corner of the field and so out to a little lane.

A tiny picturesque weatherboarded inn, oddly named The Cabinet, lies to the right and the church, of Saxon foundation, is worth a detour, but for the ramble route turn leftwards.

Cross a transverse lane and pass through a field gate. Keep straight on by a track with a hedge on the right, and soon reach a lane in which turn leftwards. In just over 100 yards turn rightwards over a little culvert and on to a footpath signposted to Royston, 2½ miles.

A forward slight bank of earth (albeit, after winter ploughing of adjacent fields, somewhat flattened) soon gives positive direction and

11

on breasting a rise, a fine view extending into Cambridgeshire opens out. The track becomes better defined—though the ground slopes sideways under your feet.

Continue forward now on a rather slender path (always forward) alongside a hedge. You emerge on a clear rubble track and keep forward passing, on your left, the buildings of Hatchpen. Shortly after passing these, the brick tower of Mile End Farm windmill can be seen over to your left. The conical roof does not appear to be the original cap but was probably put on to convert the otherwise disused mill into a store.

Keep straight on, however. You might find, later, that part of the forward way has been ploughed up, but as this right of way is much used by horse-riders it usually gets reinstated.

So, always forward, you come to The Grange. Go up the drive and, through a gateway at its head, turn rightwards over the grass and then left. Then on a clear track resume your previous forward way, ie you have made an anti-clockwise half circle around the farm.

Keep straight on over a cross-track; your route subsequently becomes first a rough little lane and then a newly residential one. It comes out on Barkway Street. Here either (a) turn left, soon to reach the main car park again or (b) turn left, but soon turn rightwards in Priory Lane, past the police station and then make a left turn to the often much-animated Market Square. Here turn rightwards down Market Hill and so to the crossroads at the town centre with the rather coy entrance to Royston Cave almost opposite.

Walk 2

**Baldock, Clothall
and Weston**

8 miles (13 km)

OS sheet 166

Baldock is just off the A1(M). Branch off on the A6141 2 miles south of the town. Park in one of the car parks in the High Street, Whitehorse Street or Church Street.

Hill names are prolific hereabouts: for example Windmill Hill, Ashanger Hill, Hickmans Hill and the Weston Hills. They are gentle and Down-like, but command good views over the Cambridgeshire plain. Weston (and the Weston Giant) will be mentioned in connection with the next walk.

From the town centre go along Whitehorse Street and continue over crossroads along the Royston Road. A few yards after passing Grosvenor Road (on the right) turn rightwards on a little lane by a red brick house named 'California'. On soon reaching a house named 'Windrush' keep forward, now by footpath with a garden wall on your immediate left. For a few yards the path/track may be vague, but you soon shift a trifle left (up a slight embankment) and at once resume your forward way, now by a good track. Down-like country stretches ahead and away to your right you will see the Weston Hills over which you will return.

Keep on over one crossing road. Where a road slants in from the right, keep forward. On reaching a modernized farm shed (seen prominently ahead) turn rightwards on a track with, at first, a hedge on your right. A little later, shift so as to have the hedge on your left. And so out to a road in which turn left. Soon slant off half right on a signposted hedged bridleway. Follow this clear bridleway for about a mile until you reach cottages at Hickmans Hill.

Here (if you do not want to visit Clothall church) you can keep straight on, and soon, after disregarding a right-hand turn, be on a magnificent green track. Otherwise turn squarely left at the first offshoot. When, after passing some housing, the lane bends rightwards you will see a path on the left (point X) which will take you to the finely-placed church. If it is open you might find some brass-rubbers industriously at work and see much else of interest. But even if the church is closed, the view from the churchyard, over the cornfields to Baldock, is most enjoyable.

Return to point X and continue round the bend in the lane. Very soon, however, take the right-hand lane at the end of which

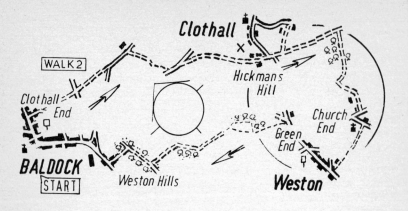

there once stood a remarkably isolated inn (the Barley Mow), now, alas, closed these past few years. Canned drinks and a picnic lunch are indicated. On reaching the lonely lane end turn right and then turn left and follow out the green lane which ensues. It can be rather muddy and is much used by the local cavalry, but there is a 'side' way which might be used discreetly. And so you come out on the broad green lane again and turn left, joining those who have come straight on from Hickmans Hill. (I have to point out, however, that this track from the pub is not, apparently, a public right of way but probably permissive only. Yet I have never seen any 'Private' notice. You could, of course, always retrace your way from Clothall church via Hickmans Hill.)

Keep on the magnificent green lane for about ¼ mile looking carefully (just after passing a hut) for the start of a line of woodland striking off on the right. Immediately past this, turn rightwards on to a track and go with the trees on your right. Continue through a woodland belt and keep ahead on another track.

A little more than halfway down the right-hand side of this field where the wire ends and the ditch goes through a culvert (just before a large tree) one should technically strike off half right. But this path for many a long year has ceased to have any physical existence. So we might take the way favoured by local horse-riders.

Just keep on the track, to the field end where, instead of going through a gate, turn very sharply right on a green way (almost doubling on your tracks). In 100 yards turn sharply left on a track, passing a water tank on your left. The narrow, rising, hedged track is followed to, and left of, a farm after which it becomes drive-like.

On reaching a road turn rightwards for about 50 yards and then turn left in the church drive. Enter Weston churchyard through the lychgate at once passing, on your left, the alleged grave of the Weston Giant. Soon after passing the church porch veer half left to a

14

maroon-coloured gate in the corner of the churchyard and so get on to a clear hedged path.

Where this subsequently turns rightwards, keep straight on now along the edge of a playing field and maintain this direction in the next field, parallel at first to the left-hand fence but then bearing half right as farm buildings are approached and so, by a short enclosed section, out, opposite the Red Lion to crossroads in Weston centre.

Turn right and fork left so as to pass the green and pond on your right.

Just past the White Horse disregard a left-hand lane. Keep on, past Darnalls Hall Farm. Where (at Green End) the road bends rightwards, turn squarely left on a footpath (disregarding the enticing broad trackway). In the first two meadows (really, I think, subdivisions of the erstwhile one field still shown on current OS maps) one keeps by or near the left-hand hedge. In the next small field one makes for a stile a little to the right of the left-hand corner. In the next field cut across (it isn't far to go) to reach a corner of a square projection of woodland.

Have this on your right but at the next corner, in lieu of a ploughed-out path forward, it may be better (and presumably the farmer wants it this way) to turn rightwards and go round the woodland 'bay' where may be a path of sorts. Do not enter the wood at all. So you come to and cross a footbridge spanning a deep ditch. The ensuing path (ploughed but usually quickly re-made) cuts a small corner of a field. You now have your reward in finding yourself on a good clear track which runs to a triangular wood which you pass on your left, disregarding a leftward track. A little later disregard another left-hand track and continue forward, the way becoming footpath-like.

So you come to a transverse woodland façade. Enter the woodland and at once turn rightwards on a clear track/path which runs just inside the edge of the wood. Quite soon turn left on a path through the trees and on leaving the wood keep forward by the residential Woodland Way soon out to the London Road in which turn right-wards. Before long you will have the still-remaining Georgian charm of old Baldock to beguile this road stretch. And so back to your parked car.

Walk 3

Weston, Chesfield and Friends Green

5 miles (8 km)

OS sheet 166

One way of reaching our starting point would be to take the A1(M) to the interchange just short of Letchworth. Here turn east on the A6141 but leave this, almost at once, on the B197. Again, leave this very soon for the minor, un-numbered lane eastwards into Weston and park discreetly in the village.

Weston, with its willow-fringed duck pond on the green and with some attractive inns, is a pleasant village: a good example of the type of starting point easy to reach by car but very inconvenient by public transport.

The church is older, and far more interesting inside, than its bleak exterior would lead you to expect. In a corner of the church-yard 'Jack O' Legs' is said to be buried. He was a Robin Hood type, of giant stature, so tall that even though the head and foot stones of the grave are 14 ft apart, Jack had to be doubled up before they could get him in, or so the story goes.

Cynics — the type of people who tell innocent children that 'there ain't no Santa Claus' — would have us believe that Jack was a mere legend and that the alleged head and foot stones are really simple stones marking two entirely separate, humble graves. Another illusion shattered! But go and see for yourself. After entering the churchyard by this route, pass the church door on your left. Just before leaving the churchyard, by the lych gate, you'll see the 'grave' on the right.

Chesfield is one of the now-vanished villages of Herts. The church which once served its community is now a roofless ruin standing in a farm yard. Especially when the trees are bare, it can be seen quite easily from the public way so please do not trespass.

From Weston centre go along the Damask Green Road, passing the Thatched House pub and also the fork (which you ignore) for the Weston Park Scout Camp. In just over ¼ mile past this you will see a public footpath signpost, for Gravely, on the right (point X). Turn in here, by some sheep pens, soon to reach an old iron swing gate. Here turn squarely left with a hedge and before long, a bit of woodland on your left. There is a definite field-edge footpath though in high summer it can be grassy and scrubby in places. At the field end turn a few yards rightwards to a gate gap (point Y). Go through

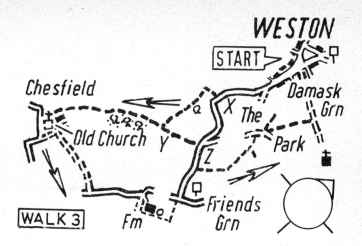

it and turn rightwards with a hedge on your right.

For a slightly easier route you could continue in the lane to point Z, opposite a drive, and turn in rightwards here (see map).

The field-edge path from point Z brings you to a small wooden field gate. Through this, cross a field, somewhat half left, to the iron field gate in view. This is followed in a few yards, by another. Then, with a wood on your left, pass through double wooden gates. As this is horse-paddock country it would be more tactful to climb over the gates (at the hinge end, please) rather than untie them. Finally, with a farm fence on your left come out to an angle of lane. Here turn sharp left.

At the point where the lane itself turns squarely right, turn left in a drive. Just beyond an old chalk pit, and at fuel tanks, turn in rightwards, practically opposite Chesfield old church ruins.

The ensuing track goes via a field gate with a hedge and wire on your right, out, via another gate, to a lane. Turn left. In rather over ¼ mile turn rightwards on to a drive at Tilekiln Farm. There is a bar stile to use should the way have a cattle barrier across it.

At once take the right-hand (forward) concreted track. Turn left with it. After passing farm buildings and a pond, keep by the left-hand hedge. Immediately before the first transverse field gate turn left with a hedge on the right. So to the Anchor at Friends Green.

Continue in the Weston Road. In less than ¼ mile, immediately past Friends Green Farm, get over a stile on the right. Slant over to the left-hand fence. After getting over bars in the subsequent corner note that ahead over the parkland you see two oval clumps of trees. Make for the right-hand end of the left-hand clump. Continue your direction so as to join a drive at the point where the right-hand woodland façade you have gradually approached, meets it.

Cross and note, half right, there is a large greenhouse ahead.

17

Right of this is a cottage. And right of this is a conspicuous white gate. Make for this and so reach a junction of drives. Maintain your direction to another, similar, gate. Your path is as a bowstring to the bow of the hutments of the scout camp. Just to the right of the flagstaff is a gate in the boundary fence. By a short woodland path you then continue ahead, with wire on the left, to a stile giving on to a neat enclosed path.

For a visit to Weston church turn right but for the ramble route, turn left. Soon go forward through a wooden swing gate and along the left-hand edge of a playing field. Leave by another swing gate and carry on ahead, parallel at first, to a wire fence but then half right to a tall wooden swing gate just to the left of the farm ahead. So, by a short enclosed path, back to Weston again.

Walk 4

Great Offley, The Icknield Way and Lilley Hoo

6 miles (10 km)

OS sheet 166

Since it has recently been bypassed, Great Offley lies just off the A505 about halfway between Hitchin and Luton.

There appears to be no official parking place though pub parking is possible by arrangement. School Lane seems too narrow for safe parking, but the High Street towards the church is better. There is a very limited parking space at the north-east end of the Icknield Way but, especially at fine weekends, it is likely to be fully taken up.

This is John Bunyan country. Two things require some effort, nowadays, to appreciate. First, we are free to profess any (or no) religion but in Bunyan's time it was dangerous not to conform. John suffered long imprisonment on this account. On his many preaching tours he was compelled to hold clandestine meetings—in remote woodland dells and by night. Secondly, John (1628-88) did not have the advantage of package holidays to far-off places, nor TV travelogues and the like. So far as I know he never saw an English mountain. His topographical inspiration for *The Pilgrim's Progress* came from local sources. Seen from his native Bedfordshire plain, the Chiltern escarpment we walk today was most likely a model for his 'Delectable Mountains'.

Telegraph Hill is probably named from a semaphore (like an old-type railway signal) which stood on this 600-ft height, one of a chain used to signal (possibly) defence intelligence in pre-electric days.

Whilst Offley is well supplied with inns there are no pubs actually on this round so a picnic lunch and canned drinks are indicated.

From the crossroads in Offley centre go up School Lane, disregarding a left-hand branch. Go over the bypass in its deep cutting and curve leftwards with the lane, ignoring any bridleway offshoots.

At guideposts, where the drive for Little Offley goes forward, veer half right, for Wellbury House. A little later, at a fork, bear half right, disregarding the forward private way. The surfaced drive is followed to the outskirts of Wellbury House School and is then continued as a more stony track. It is a pedestrian right-of-way. So you follow out, past a pretty thatched cottage and with a fine view of Deacon Hill over to your left, to the B655 and turn left.

Just past the 'Bedfordshire' sign, turn left on a well-defined track. It is a well-preserved section of the ancient Icknield Way.

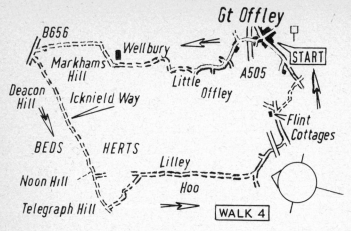

Some years ago barrier posts were set up in an attempt to keep out the diddicoy element who were leaving their litter here but, unfortunately, it takes more than a few posts to prevent this sort of thing. However, you soon pass this unsightly area and the way becomes sweet and clean and makes for ideal walking.

With your right foot in Bedfordshire and your left foot in Hertfordshire, since the county boundary runs down the centre of the track, you gradually rise. Deacon Hill is passed on the right and the track subsequently becomes tree-lined. A gate gap will, in due course, be noticed on the right. Disregard this. But go through the next one, about 1¼ miles from the start of the track. As a check on your position note that if you come to a public bridleway sign on the left you have gone about 60 steps too far.

If you have turned into the field just mentioned, and have your back to the Icknield Way, the theoretical right of way is, I believe, now half rightwards across a field to a stile gap. In actual practice, since the original path has long lapsed, you go *forward* to a hedged corner. On my survey visit I found a marked path. On reaching the corner just mentioned turn rightwards with the hedge and fence on your left. You soon come to a gap which once held a stile. The short section from the corner to the stile gap must be presumed to be a permissive diversion of the old diagonal path. I found it well used.

Beyond this a magnificent view meets the eye. You are on an escarpment overlooking an extensive plain, with a deep coombe immediately below. Return the same way and resume your previous forward way along the old track and so to the summit of Telegraph Hill and then start descending. Very soon turn left on a clear sign-posted trackway. Follow it out, later round a half-right bend. The prospect is even more lovely when you have passed the power lines. So you traverse Lilley Hoo ('Hoo' meaning 'headland') until, in just under 1½ miles from Telegraph Hill, and with a slight left curve, you come to the head of a more surfaced lane.

20

Continue down this, under the new bypass, to the old main road in which turn left. After passing a farm on the right you come to Flint Cottages on the left. Opposite these take a signposted bridle-way out to a lane in which turn left. At Claypits Cottages, the old main road (much quieter than it was!) is rejoined and followed into Great Offley.

Walk 5

Great Offley, Preston and Charlton

10 or 8 miles (16 or 13 km)

OS sheet 166

Great Offley lies just off the A505 about half way between Hitchin and Luton. There appears to be no official parking place. School Lane seems too narrow to be parked in safely; maybe the High Street, towards the church, is better.

John Bunyan has already been mentioned in the previous walk; you may care to glance at this. On this round we pass by a cottage (modernized but still retaining much old-world charm) where Bunyan lodged on one of his many preaching tours in this area. We also pass through Wain Wood where in one of the dells here John held a clandestine midnight prayer meeting.

On all of my previous visits to the wood I have found it in its 'natural' state but one must realize that wood is often a crop which must be harvested when it is mature. So one of these days I suppose I will find the wood cleared and replanted.

From Great Offley village centre go down the High Street, passing the church on your left. At the Red Lion turn leftwards on a minor road (soon track-like). Where this turns squarely left *keep straight on* by a grassy track, open on the left, a hedge on the right. It is continued (disregard a left and then a right fork) ahead as an open cart track to reach a woodland corner.

Have the wood on your left for a few yards and then slant off half rightwards on what I found to be a clear open track (but it could, of course, be ploughed). Over the field, turn to have a hedge, concealing a wood, on your left. Keep ahead ignoring, in a field corner, a track into the wood. The bracken-lined way, always with a hedge on your left, becomes more footpath-like and brings you out at a tiny cluster of cottages which make up Austage End. Turn left. In a few yards one meets, at point A on the map, a footpath signpost.

For Preston you should turn rightwards at point A. It is possible however, after much rain or after a season of lush growth, that this A-B branch is not to your liking. Should this be the case, just use the C-D branch.

For this, ignore the signposted track (point A) just mentioned. Keep ahead by the wide track for 300 yards and immediately after passing through a field gate opening, turn rightwards on a

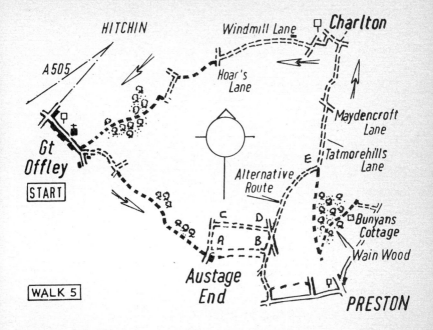

pleasant track, fenced on the right, open on the left, and follow it out to a road.

On reaching the road at once turn rightwards along the edge of the grass verge and continue (V-wise from the road) along a splendid green lane; soon passing point B. A little later ignore (on the right) another branch. Now keep an eye open for a stile on the left which comes 300 yards later. Over this continue with a hedge on your left and then by a line of trees. You pass just left of a wooden shed and rightwards of the Pond Farm buildings after which the meadow path bears half rightwards down to a lane opposite a house named 'Little Kendals'.

Here turn rightwards and at the crossroads, left. So you arrive at Preston.

Take, now the Hitchin road, not Chequers Lane. In ½ mile turn left on a tiny signposted byway. After this has bent half left, do not take the obviously private drive to Bunyan's Cottage but take the track so as to pass the back of the cottage on your left. You can get a glimpse of the front of the cottage from the foot of the drive; please do not trespass. Follow the path through Wain Wood and on emerging, turn rightwards with the wood on your right and open fields on your left. A little later you have a bit of woodland on the left also. Maintain your direction, now passing an old chalk pit on the left to emerge on a field where, forward, you continue with a

23

hedge on your right and so emerge (at point E) on to a hedged green track (Tatmorehills Lane) and follow it down to, and over, a transverse little road called Maydencroft Lane.

The track—which can be muddy!—takes a double bend and brings you to a transverse little lane. Here turn left. If the little lane is followed out it will bring you to the Windmill at Charlton. But for the ramble route, turn left at the thatched cottage, then right and, in the main road reached, turn left.

Very soon turn rightwards on a farm road which, past a farm, becomes a track with a hedge on the right. You subsequently come to a spot where, unless horse-riders have remade the track, your forward way (the true line of the public footpath) is ploughed out. You will find, however, that the farmer has provided a little detour anticlockwise around the rectangular wooded 'bay'.

You come out on a narrow hedged track (Hoar's Lane). Cross to a field-edge footpath opposite, with a hedge on the footpath left. This gradually gets better marked. On reaching a track corner turn squarely left. Where the track turns sharply left, turn squarely *right*. Go with the hedge on the left, soon round a left-hand bend. You then have (but not for long) the end of a plantation on your right. On coming out through a gap into a field you should, technically, bear half right to go uphill with the long flank of a wood on your left. In practice one usually goes round the corner of the field.

At the top of the wood veer half left along a rutted track, now quitting the wood and going along the right-hand edge of fields. There the track bends sharply away, continue forward by a path enclosed between hedges and so out to the Red Lion at Offley again.

Walk 6

Benington, Bassus Green and Walkern

6 miles (10 km)

OS sheet 166

Benington lies about 4 miles east of Stevenage New Town. One way of getting there is to branch rightwards off the A602 at the north-west end of Watton-at-Stone. Take, subsequently, the first right-hand turn but disregard the next right-hand offshoot. Then keep straight on.

Park discreetly; near the village hall perhaps.

If a contest were held to decide which was the most picturesque Hertfordshire village Benington would, without the slightest doubt, reach the finals and have a good chance of being awarded the first prize.

Walkern, a larger village, still retains its charm though it is only just over the hill from latter-day Stevenage. The dovehouse will attract photographers though the best view is obtained by facing west (which means that morning light is essential). As this is a circular walk, there is nothing to stop you basing the walk on Walkern (here again, the usual discreet street parking).

From the pond at Benington Green go along Duck Lane. In ¼ mile, opposite a white-railed cottage, get over a stile on the left. Cross a meadow, via an intermediate partition fence, keeping parallel to the right-hand hedge. By a stile you emerge onto a little lane and turn left. At a thatched house at the corner turn right. In 300 yards turn rightwards on a concreted drive.

Where this veers half-right to enter the private grounds of Walkern Hall keep straight on, soon to reach a road. Here turn right and, very soon, left, through the farmyard. Keep straight on by a rough track. You enter a field and keep on by the right-hand edge. From a field gate in the dip, the way is continued forward as a grassy track which subsequently reaches a lane in which you turn left, past a few scattered cottages which make up Bassus Green.

At the crossroads keep straight on (no through road). Immed-iately after passing a large dutch barn on the left, and by some cylindrical storage tanks, turn left. Slant over a transverse farm road and go by the downhill gravelled track, open on the left and with a hedgeback on the right.

In the dip turn leftwards on what proves to be a splendid track, sufficiently used by farm vehicles, horse-riders and (one hopes!)

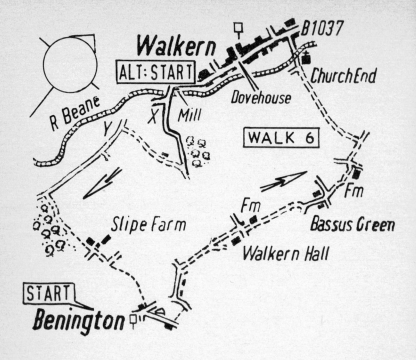

ramblers to keep the grass down. It is followed out, past the church (which has been a landmark), now as a lane and over the Beane ford to emerge on the High Street of Walkern. Here turn left passing a dovehouse on your right. At Walkern, about 3 miles from the start, is a choice of inns.

Keep straight on through the village and just past the restored flour mill you reach the war memorial. Here (point X) you could keep straight on in the road to point Y but the following detour is recommended.

At the war memorial turn left, uphill. Note, a little later, that a wood starts on your left. A couple of hundred yards past this point (⅜ mile from the memorial) slant back sharply right on a clear gravelled track. As you descend there is a superb view of the Beane valley. It is difficult to believe that the sprawl of Stevenage New Town lies just over the skyline.

On reaching the road (point Y) turn left. Disregard the first left-hand offshoot but ⅜ mile past this, on reaching a pair of footpath signposts on either side of the road, turn leftwards on a trackway. At the fork soon met *do not veer half right into the wood*. Keep straight ahead on the fieldside path with the wood on your immediate right. You continue by a woodland track. I hope you do not find it too overgrown but it is quite short and soon brings you to a wooden field gate with a stile adjacent.

26

Keep on with the wood now again on your right. Slipe Farm then comes into view. Cross to a barn and pass this on your immediate left. Disregard the left-hand offshoot. Where, in a few more yards, the concreted track swings rightwards, *keep straight on*, through a field gate, now by a gravelled track. Just before this swings left get over a stile on the right and immediately turn left, with the hedge on your left.

In the field corner you come to a stile and footplanks. Over these you come to a field. Proceed diagonally to the top right-hand corner. (If the field should be in plough a round-the-field-edge route might be considered.) Over wooden bars continue with trees on your right.

Benington village hall soon comes in sight. Go to the left-hand end of the surrounding fence and so out to a road in which turn rightwards to Benington centre again.

Walk 7

Knebworth Park, Langley and Drivers End

6 miles (10 km)

OS sheet 166

If you intend to park in Knebworth Park (see notes which follow) you can reach the motorists' park entrance by the new road which slants back from the A1(M) shortly before reaching Stevenage. For discreet lane parking at other places I can only suggest a study of the sketch map in conjunction with a touring map which most motorists carry.

In originally planning this route I intended to park the car at Langley and to start the walk from there. But this hamlet stands in a cul-de-sac with very little public parking space and parking on the main road cannot be encouraged. If you come this way during winter months when Knebworth House and its pleasure grounds are closed, some discreet parking on the circular route will be found. Otherwise, if Knebworth House is open, it would be better to pay for admission and park there.

Knebworth House, home of the Lyttons, and the park are the obvious draw. It should be explained that several public rights of way traverse Knebworth Park and are always open. It is these we use on this walk. We must keep strictly to them. But if we have paid for admission we can wander practically at will. Users of Knebworth Park footpaths should note that maintenance work is constantly going on. So be prepared for any changes in the description of fences, gates and stiles here.

Standing in the car park of Knebworth Park, a little rightwards of and with your back to the Barn, you will be facing an avenue. Go up this and, where it soon turns right, continue forward over the grass to a ladder stile. Without crossing this (but see note at end) turn left, keeping to the right-hand fence, soon veering to and crossing a low dam. Beyond this pass through a gate and turn right. You come, in a few yards, to a notice board. Continue a few more yards and then turn left. The 'waymarks' on the trees which once made the way clear were, on my visit, very much faded. But look for them. You should finally emerge from the wood at a corner. If not, correct your position.

Keep *forward*, disregarding the horse-riders' trail rightwards. Go via a field gate through the farmyard out to a farm road. Cross to the stile opposite and keep ahead over the meadow, passing a copse on your left.

28

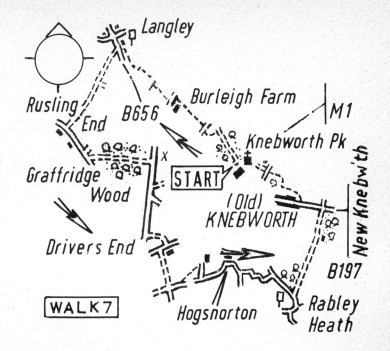

Go on by a slender path to the field bottom. Here turn rightwards for a few yards and then left, up a long narrow field, to a stile seen ahead.

Keep by the left-hand hedge and after passing garages turn left in a rough little track out to the Hitchin Road B656. There used to be a transport café here. Unfortunately it is now closed.

Opposite this take the footpath signposted for Rusling End. It goes at first parallel to the wood over on your right and runs with the power line for company. Subsequently, after going through a field gate slant half right to farm sheds and so out to a lane in which turn left through Rusling End which is just a few cottages. Immediately *after* the lane has bent rightwards take a track on the left through Graffridge Wood.

This brings you out to the B656 again (point X). For a quick return to the start, cross to the path opposite (to the right of cottages) and, over a ladder stile take a path over the parkland, more or less square with the road just quitted. On joining a 'made' drive turn left and follow it back to the car park.

For the full walk, however, turn rightwards on the B656 and disregard first a right-hand turn and then a left-hand one. In just over ¼ mile after this, turn left on a drive and follow out to a crosslane. Turn right for about 50 yards and then left by the side of the 'Node Dairy Farm' which may be described as 'more Hollywood than Herts'. On reaching a lane turn left. In 150 yards or so (in lieu of keeping on the road — see my map) get over wooden rails and (left) take the signposted path diagonally over a rising meadow with the lane you have just left receding to the right.

Pass a midfield clump of small trees on your right. By a stile and then a field gate you come out on a road in which turn rightwards. At the T-junction turn left.

At the square right bend then met stands Hogsnorton. Take the next left-hand turn. At the T-junction turn right with a wood on your left. Just as cottages start note a signposted track on the left. This is to be taken but note that just ahead, round the bend at Rabley Heath (though there is no heath here nowadays) stands the Robin Hood and Little John — a pub with a nice garden.

But having taken the track just mentioned, we find that it leads us, roughly at first, with a wood on the left, then through woods, out to a road in which turn left. Housing then begins. By the telephone box turn rightwards to a playing field. Slant across to the children's swings. Turn rightwards with a wood on your left. At its corner turn left and follow out to a lane.

Across this, enter Knebworth Park by a public footpath. Follow a drive to the church and enter the churchyard. At the tower turn left through a gate in the deer fencing and, with a slight rightward inclination, go forward to meet a drive junction which is where we came in — at the car park and start of a rightward avenue.

Note If you *do* cross the ladder stile and go forward (you'll be on a public right of way) for a short distance, you can get a glimpse of the lake. Return and proceed with main ramble.

Walk 8

Waterford, Stapleford and Watton-at-Stone

9 miles (14 km)

OS sheet 166

Waterford is on the A602 a few miles out of Hertford.

Park discreetly off the main road. At fine summer weekends be prepared for a fair number of visitors to this popular riverside spot.

The interest of the little River Beane (also to be encountered in Walk 14) is a special feature of this walk. The river joins the Lea at Hertford. The places names *Waterford* and *Stapleford* are significant.

Opposite the Waterford Arms go up the lane and over the Beane. Very soon turn leftwards on the residential Barley Croft. Where this soon ends, bend left at the last left-hand house, to a stile. Then go across a meadow to the railway arch seen ahead. Keep on by the leafy track, with the river to the left, until you come out, quite suddenly, to a road. So be very careful if you have venturesome children or dogs racing ahead!

Turn left and at once disregard a left-hand lane. You pass Bullsmill Farm and its silos on your left and disregard a right-hand turning. Immediately the farm buildings end you should, in theory, get over a small stile set in the angle of fence on your left and cross the field diagonally to a stile in the corner. The usual practice for some time past has been to ignore this stile and to continue in the farm road a little farther then to take a path on the left.

Either way you reach the river (this will be on your left) and you follow its leafy banks all the way to Stapleford church. Turn rightwards in the winding narrow uphill road to a junction. For the ramble route turn *left* but if, at this stage, you require an inn, take the path forward across the field to the Three Harts (see Walk 14) which can be seen ahead and afterwards return.

Having turned left at the junction as just described, you subsequently pass cottages and a farm and are then in Woodhall Park domain. After you have crossed a minor tributary of the Beane turn left passing Home Farm, with its prominent silos, on your immediate right. Where the buildings end turn leftwards over a bridge at a lakehead, a damming and widening of the Beane. Then bear rightwards in the drive out, by a lodge, on to the main road. Here turn rightwards.

At the first left-hand turning on the outskirts of Watton-at-Stone

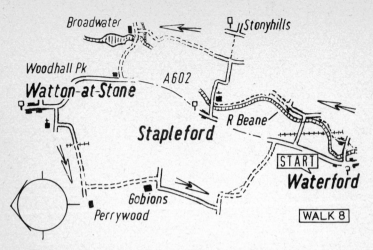

proceed to the church. Opposite this take a lane, for Perrywood. This quiet drive-like byway takes you over the railway and in ½ mile farther you come to a cottage on the left. Immediately beyond this turn leftwards on a fine, signposted bridleway and follow it out for ½ mile or so to a lane. Here turn right for a few yards and then left.

This lane, slightly downhill and with wide views ahead, brings you to what appears to be a transverse road; actually it is a point where the 'made' road you have been using turns squarely right and a gravelly track, which you take, turns squarely left.

This farm road bends rightwards and then bears left. From the map you will see that at one point the public path cuts a corner of the way. But this is extremely theoretical nowadays. You follow out the track to the main road again and can either follow it (rightwards) directly into Waterford or take the first left-hand turning and retrace a trifle of your outward way.

Note (if you haven't done Walk 14) that opposite the start of Barley Croft an iron swing gate gives access to a very pleasant Beane-side path.

Walk 9

**Kimpton and Ayot
St Lawrence**

5½ miles (9 km)

OS sheet 166

Kimpton lies at the intersection of the B651 running north from
St Albans via Sandridge and Wheathampstead and the B652
running north-east from Harpenden. One could also reach it (but
read your map correctly) by branching west from the B656 at
Codicote.

Discreet parking in the area by the church is possible.

Kimpton lies in a western Hertfordshire valley near the Bedfordshire border. (One may presume that many of the occupants of
the newer part of the village are commuters to Luton.) The interesting church with its tiny lead spire is seen to good advantage from
the higher ground at the initial stages of this walk.

Our base is the Boot at Kimpton. With your back to the inn go
leftwards (eastward). Ignore the first left-hand offshoot but take the
next (right-hand) one. The rising land here is Ballsclough Hill. As
you ascend out of the valley, look back at the village, and the
church, below.

In ⅜ mile the lane bends squarely rightwards. At this point leave
it and go leftwards on a rough cart track.

This, soon gently descending, is subsequently continued as a footpath which takes you through fir plantations and, a few stiles later,
emerges on to parkland. Keep ahead with the fenced-off woodland
on your right to a corner (point X).

Now, if you do not want to visit Ayot St Lawrence (some notes on
which you will find within Walk 13) and its inn, you can, at this
point, turn very acutely left (V-fashion). Then pick up the ramble
route from the description which soon follows.

To reach Ayot St Lawrence you may possibly have to get through a
'fall down' wire gate which confronts you. These are an anathema to
ramblers who would like to co-operate with the farmer in preventing
his cattle straying, but find it difficult to operate gates of the type
just mentioned. All too often the fastening loops are so tight that
refastening calls for great strength. And, on my original visit, I found
that the fastening loops were themselves of barbed wire — a danger to
the hands.

Assuming things have improved by the time you come this way and
and you have got over the 'gate', at once turn left on a transverse

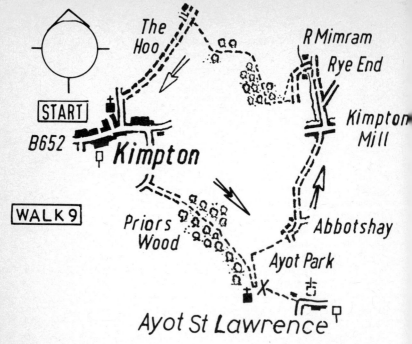

enclosed path and go over a stile. Ignore (at least for the main ramble route) the entry into the churchyard of Ayot St Lawrence 'new' church and from a forward swing gate continue with a plain wire fence on your left.

If you cannot negotiate the wire gate, just turn leftwards (without getting over it) with the fence (and enclosed path on the other side) on your right. You soon come to the smooth wire fence just mentioned. This is easily stepped over.

Either way, follow the wire fence to cottages at a lane corner where turn left to the old, ruined, church and the recently refurbished Brocket Arms.

Having, possibly, refreshed yourself, retrace your way to point X. Slant gradually away from the left-hand wooded edge. No marked path shows on the grass but you should soon reach a stile. Look for it ahead or scout around if you at first miss it. It comes about ¼ mile from the V turn.

Over this stile turn rightwards and follow the right-hand hedge out to a little lane in which keep forward, passing a large house with its stables and outbuildings. This is 'Abbotshay' although I did not see the name marked up. Just beyond where the lane bends a little rightwards, keep *forward*, now by a track which is nominally signposted though on my original visit I found the signpost collapsed. As I do not include a post-holer in my rucksack I had to be content with propping up the post as best I could.

The point to remember is to keep, now, always *forward*, ignoring any left-hand branches. The true way, I suppose, is along the hollow overgrown way. Thus the permissive field-edge substitute path alongside is, at first, narrow, but adequate for most walkers. The track widens as it runs downhill and offers good views.

On reaching a lane, where the path you have come by is signposted, cross to, and go up, a lane practically opposite. At this corner, where the river Mimram makes a square bend, was an old water mill, proof that, in former times, there was sufficient water in the river here to work the wheel profitably. Now, except after unusually rainy periods, there is only a modest flow—a circumstance which I have noted in other rambles (eg 10 and 11). Can it be that the 'little rivers' which once served local needs are being sacrificed to the ever-increasing demands of more distant large towns?

Very soon, at a right-hand bend, keep *forward* on a gravelly farm road. On reaching the first (Rye End) cottages turn left, over the stripling Mimram. Disregard the obviously private left fork to Rye End Farm. You curve round the farm to go squarely rightwards and then squarely left. If the narrow field to the right of the farm road ahead is in grass, go diagonally across it to a gate in the far corner. But should it be ploughed, continue along the farm road (you'll still be on a right of way) and immediately before the next gate turn rightwards over (as I found) sacking-covered barbed wire and go along the field-end to a gate near the left-hand corner.

Through this gate proceed with a wood on your immediate right. In the field corner turn rightwards through a field gate on to a track between two woods, the right-hand of which soon ends; you continue with the other on your left. At the top go through a gate on the left and continue by the left-hand hedge to have, in the next field, a wood on your immediate right.

You then go through a gate and proceed with a young fir plantation on your left. Finally go half left over a large park-like meadow to arrive at a drive opposite Hoo Park Cottage.

Turn left in this drive, downhill to a lane where turn left. A couple of hundred yards later turn rightwards through the churchyard and then leftwards, back to Kimpton centre.

Walk 10

Welwyn North, Harmer Green and Tewin

8 miles (13 km)

OS sheet 166

As this is a circular walk it could equally well be started at Tewin, but on account of a car park I have chosen Welwyn North station as the start for purposes of description. Reach it by branching off the A1(M) just past Welwyn Garden City along the B1000 and just after passing under the viaduct, turn leftwards.

There is a car park (at BR charges!) outside Welwyn North station. At Tewin there is some parking space beside the village hall and at the Rose and Crown.

The river Lea appears, in its lower reaches, to be a somewhat work-a-day industrialized river: plebeian, in fact. One of its tributaries, the Mimram, can be accounted quite an aristocratic stream, however, since it flows through a number of fine parks in mid-Hertfordshire.

In places one is reminded of Tennyson's Brook ('I linger by my shingly bars; I loiter by my cresses ...') Yet the now-quiet Tewin Mill we pass on this walk must have formerly echoed with the clack of the mill wheel and the rumble of farm carts arriving with loads of corn to be ground.

Apart from considerable rural and photogenic charm you will see some interesting bits of industrial archaeology (a 'with-it' subject nowadays). Except for one very short section (in which it is possible to detour) all is very easy going.

The interest begins, in fact, even before you reach the start of the walk. Around 1844 the London-Peterborough-York railway was planned to run via Hitchin along the Mimram Valley. Lord Dacre of Kimpton Hoo Park (which we cross in Walk 9) successfully objected. So the railway had to go via Knebworth and Stevenage which meant crossing the Mimram by an impressive viaduct (which you see on this walk) at Digswell. Half a century later, rather than widen the viaduct to accommodate increased traffic, a loop line was built from Stevenage through Hertford, Enfield and Wood Green.

There is also a 'ha-ha' (a kind of dry moat which, whilst stopping cattle, does not impede the view from the house as a fence would) at Marden Hill and another bit of industrial archaeology — a hydraulic ram — nearby.

In Tewin churchyard is the famous tomb of Lady Ann Grimston. This lady was supposed, on her deathbed, agnostically to have

36

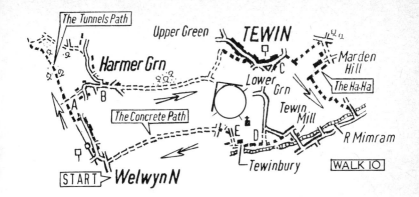

denied the doctrine of a Life Hereafter and said if she were wrong then let trees split her grave asunder. As you see, they did. Which only goes to prove that a picturesque legend and one not unique to Tewin divorced from all actual fact (the lady was reputedly as pious as any) helps to enliven many an otherwise dull guide book. If detouring from this walk, enter the churchyard, go through newer part of churchyard, circle church on your left and the railed-off tomb is near the far right-hand corner.

If you elect to start from the 'pay the porter' car park in the fore-court of Welwyn North station turn left in Harmer Green Lane, ignoring the road opposite. In a short ¼ mile go up steps, left (easily missed!) and then rightwards by garden fencing. You will be walking directly over the tunnel which accounts for the ventilating shaft (most essential in steam-train days) you encounter. Don't forget to look back at the 'perspective' of railway lines.

You enter woodland. Ignore a crosspath. Subsequently you make a quick right-left turn and continue by the railway. Note the tunnel entrance dated 1850; the path you are on is locally called 'The Tunnels Path'. Another strip of woodland is entered. You pass another air shaft on the left. On drawing level with yet another (over to your right) veer a trifle leftwards and, over a stile, continue along the right-hand edge of a field, with a wood on your right, to another stile.

Just beyond this you come to a clear cross-track in which turn rightwards. Keep always forward. You are in Harmer Green Wood which was cleared and replanted a decade or more ago. On leaving it, at once disregard a left-hand track. Instead, keep forward via an intermediate stile with the wire of the pig farm on your left. Disregard a couple of left-hand tracks.

When houses appear immediately ahead veer just a trifle right-wards and so out to a lane in which turn rightwards and cross over,

37

keeping to the sidewalk.

On reaching Harmer Green, the road making a remarkable bend to avoid cutting it, veer left with the sidewalk, soon (point B) to go down Pennyfathers Lane. You pass a pretty thatched cottage and after a short enclosed section the way becomes open. It goes up and down, soon through more trees, and subsequently—a magnificent bit, this—swings in a rightward curve. On making contact with a hedge corner turn leftwards on a pretty hedged track and come out to Tewin Upper Green.

Go across the green to the road in which turn right. Opposite Orchard House turn rightwards along the left-hand edge of the Green, and by tennis courts, soon to take a very coy (look for it!) enclosed path on the left which soon runs along the backs of houses and then makes a square left turn to the road again, in which turn rightwards and so to the Rose and Crown at the Lower Green (point C), a little under 4 miles from the start.

Now take the Hertford Road. Where it bends left take the sign-posted path on the right. This goes clearly forward and then half left. Follow it up through a copse and then by the left-hand edge of a field, out to a lane. Turn right and very soon turn in rightwards on to the Marden Hill House drive. At a mini-green veer left. Then go over a few yards of grass to a prominent stile. (Do not continue leftwards in the drive.) Go forward a little but soon pass through a hedge gap and along by the 'ha-ha'.

At the transverse fence get over stile and turn left. At the field bottom get over two stiles and then turn left. After crossing the next stile you should, technically, go half right. Otherwise continue to the next corner and turn rightwards. Either way you come to the Mimram bridge. Note, industrial archaeologists, just leftwards an abandoned bit of machinery in a brick pit. The OS maps call this a 'hydraulic ram' but an engineer friend says it is a double barrel pump once worked by a paddle wheel to pump water from the river (which had a better flow formerly than it has now) to more distant parts. Its erstwhile bronze valves seem to have been knocked off in more than one sense.

On reaching the road turn right for ½ mile, disregarding, on the way, a right-hand turn for Archers Green. Turn rightwards on the Tewin Mill drive (pedestrian right of way). Over the Mimram you reach a transverse lane. Turn left. Where it bends half right keep forward by a field-edge path, with a hedge on the left. Cross a transverse track and (point D) continue (at first by the river—but note that a right of way is for passage only, not to picnic here or let the kids paddle) to a farm called Tewinbury, seen ahead. Note, on the way and to the right, the very finely placed Tewin church.

On reaching the farm turn rightwards, away from the bridge, for a few yards and then go leftwards in front of the buildings at the end of which turn squarely right on a narrow, rising, hedged track. In a couple of hundred yards or so (point E) turn left (though if you wish to visit Tewin church turn rightwards on a footpath over the field) on a track through a wood. Over a cross-lane continue by a broad track. It is believed, though some query it, that this was concreted at its edge by German POWs during World War I. Another possible explanation is that the original right of way ran past the front of Tewinwater House and that this did not please the then-owner, Sir Otto Beit, who had the path diverted to the north of, and parallel to, the old one. If so the concreting may possibly be due to the fact that a usual condition for diverting a public path is that the new way should not be less 'commodious' than the old. The original right of way lay over a firm drive, so the diversion, along an erstwhile farm track, had also to be surfaced. I have aired this question in public print many times without getting a definite answer, and I cannot completely reject the possibility that the track was part-concreted as an Estate amenity—for the benefit of private shooting parties, for example. Whatever the facts the concrete strip makes for easy going.

The latter-day skyline of Welwyn Garden City shows leftwards and the railway viaduct is impressively ahead. When you finally reach a road turn right and fork left—and so back to the car park.

Walk 11

Harpenden, Rothamsted and Redbourn

9 miles (14 km)

OS sheet 166

Harpenden—a name which, according to some authorities, is derived from 'the valley of the nightingales'—is on the A1081 26 miles from London. The walk could equally well be based on Redbourn (on the A5183).

The most convenient parking place at Harpenden for this ramble is that on the south side of Amenbury Lane. But there are others.

Rothamsted, the famous agricultural research station, is of interest on this walk. Established over a century ago by Sir John Bennet Lawes, the discoverer of superphosphates as a fertiliser, it has a fine lime avenue.

The starting point is the Harpenden Arms pub. From here go in the direction of London, on common land rightwards of the road (passing the 'village' sign). Having passed the Silver Cup, the name of which commemorates the horse races held on the common up to the time of World War I (see also note to Walk 13 regarding the Tin Pot), veer a little more rightwards along West Common. At the end of Pimlico Place (note the 1822 plaque) turn rightwards and then left on a clear, signposted path, and follow it out to Hatching Green.

Here continue forward a short distance. Avoid the private drives of Rothamsted Cottages and Rothamsted Lodge. But at Rothamsted Park Lodge turn rightwards along a signposted drive. You subsequently come to a spot (point X on the map) where a drive runs off rightwards. Turn leftwards here, through an iron swing gate with a footpath sign.

Go somewhat half left of your previous direction to an angle of fence and maintain this direction, gradually approaching (but never contacting) the iron fence over to your right. So you reach a road and turn left in it.

In about ½ mile turn rightwards on the golf club drive. Just after you have passed the end of the golf course disregard a right-hand offshoot. Instead, bear half left, passing Hammondsend Farm. Beyond this the track becomes less formal. You go round a right-left bend and come to a corner (where is a fine, wide view). Turn left here, soon with a wood on your left. Shortly after the wood ends, turn rightwards on a rutted grassy track. On reaching a prominent cross-track turn rightwards to emerge, in due course, on to a

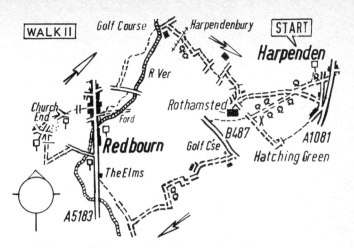

curiously bumpy field, possibly old gravel workings.

You gradually bear over to the busy Watling Street (A5183) to a stile and footpath sign, just short of a house named 'The Elms'. Avoid in this last field turning left in a cross-track.

Turn rightwards in the main road. You can follow it straight into Redbourn but a much more pleasant detour is this: At the Chequers turn left in Chequer Lane. Just before reaching the railway bridge turn left on a signposted track. Go over a little stream and then take the rightmost of two tracks. This enters a field and becomes a footpath (unploughed baulk). At the far corner go through a fence gap and at once turn sharp right.

Now with a fence on your right follow over a rail crossing to the road in which turn left. Go over crossroads and immediately after, at a Y fork, either (a) take the left-hand branch to the photogenic Church End and the Orange Tree, or (b) take the right-hand branch for a few yards and then turn rightwards on a tarmac path between trees of varying ages. Over a branch road continue forward still on the avenue (unless you wish to detour rightwards to have an innings at the appropriately named Cricketers, where on a summer Saturday or Sunday afternoon you may lazily watch cricket on Redbourn Common). You cross another road and enter an alleyway directly ahead and so come out to the High Street of Redbourn.

Cross over. Turn rightwards for only a few yards. Then go left in Waterend Lane, round a right-hand bend and almost to a ford. (It is worth continuing to this photogenic ford and then retracing your way.) But route-wise, just before reaching this ford, however, turn left on an enclosed path signposted for Harpenden Lane. At a latter-day road curve, cut across it and continue ahead, again by an enclosed path, out to a road. Here turn left. In about a couple of hundred yards, turn rightwards on a clear hedged signposted bridle-way. From the subsequent stile by a gate, continue ahead, passing a large shed on the right. A little beyond this bear rather more than

41

half right with a fence on your left. Where this bends left go only half left across the riparian meadow. Your objective is seen ahead—the mellow roof of a large old barn adjoining Harpendenbury Farm.

At a stile you enter the comparatively newly laid-out golf course. Go forward by the embankment and then over what—at least on the map—is the river Ver. Owing to a fall in the general water level the stream seems, at this point, to be completely dry nowadays. You come to a prominent cross-drive.

The farm here is Harpendenbury. Pass a corner black shed on your right and go up a little hedged lane. Very soon veer off half right on what was (on my visit) quite a prominent track; at first open and then wired off through a paddock. Go carefully, over the railway and continue with a wood on your right. In 250 yards or so, turn clearly left and soon, at a group of trees, turn right. Continue over a cross-track, now with a wire fence on your right.

At the next cross-track turn left. On reaching a drive turn right. On reaching a junction of drives, with a red-brick building ahead, turn acutely left, passing a cottage on your left. Continue by this minor drive. On reaching a fine main avenue, cross directly over and continue your quiet way absolutely straight on out to the beautiful Harpenden Common again.

Walks 12 a and b   Round about Rothamsted

OS sheet 166

Walk 12a   Harpenden, Hatching Green and Rothamsted

3 miles (5 km)

See Walk 11 for instructions on how to reach Harpenden, the starting point of this ramble, and where to park there.

Quite early in my ramble-writing career, having noticed that several of my old rambling companions, now married, were taking Junior along, first papoose-fashion in a framed carrier on Dad's back and then trundled along in a fold-up go-chair, I took the opportunity of giving, now and again, a short ramble-route which used the maximum number of reasonably smooth drives.

It was only much later that I was touched to receive a letter from a correspondent who said that he scanned my newspaper articles every week for suitable stretches over which he could wheel his wife's invalid chair.

So if you are faced with either of these two problems, this walk along the Rothamsted drives — one a glorious lime avenue — is for you. And, of course, it makes a good short walk for anyone.

Walk 12a is really a shortened form of Walk 11. To obviate the need for cross-reference the relevant instructions are repeated here and are also separately mapped. Walk 12b can be done separately or combined with Walk 12a to form a Q-shaped route. One can return to base at Harpenden either by retracing the outward route (which would give new views in, literally, a new light) over Harpenden Common or by taking an *ad lib* way over the common. (Another possibility where a small group of walkers is concerned, is that some Sir Galahad of the party — a stronger walker perhaps — will return to Harpenden to fetch the car whilst the others wait — need I suggest where — at Ayres End.)

The starting point is the Harpenden Arms pub. From here go in the direction of London over common land, rightwards of the road (passing the village sign). Having passed the Silver Cup (the name commemorates horse races held on the common up to the time of World War I: see also a note to Walk 13 regarding the Tin Pot) veer a little more rightwards along West Common. At the end of Pimlico Place (note the 1822 plaque) turn rightwards and then left

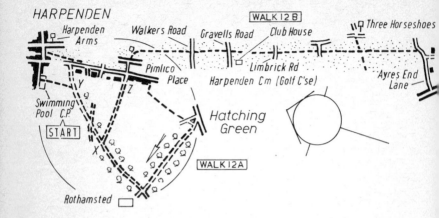

on a clear, signposted path and follow it out to Hatching Green.

Here continue forward a short distance. Avoid the private drives of Rothamsted Cottage and Rothamsted Lodge. But at Rothamsted Park Lodge turn rightwards along a signposted drive. In a short ½ mile you come to a spot where a fine lime avenue runs off rightwards.

Turn rightwards in this. In about ¼ mile you come to a right-hand branch (point X). At this point you have a choice of ways.

If connecting with Walk 12b: turn rightwards in the drive at point X and follow it out passing, en route, various College buildings, to a road at point Z. Cross to a road opposite. This soon brings you to the main road where you cross to and go down a stony track towards a cricket pavilion. Here you connect with Walk 12b.

If returning directly to Harpenden: ignore the offshoot at point X. Keep ahead and again keep ahead, soon afterwards, when a lesser drive slants obliquely across. If you are 'walking with wheels' as mentioned in the introduction to this walk, just follow out the drive to a road where turn leftwards for the Harpenden Arms. Otherwise, 200 or so yards past the drives crossing just mentioned (and at point Y) slant half left across the parkland. The swimming pool buildings give direction. So you arrive back at Amenbury Lane where, probably, you have parked the car.

Walk 12b

**Harpenden Common and
Ayres End Lane**

2 miles (3 km)

This is a 'whistle stop' kind of walk—possibly a summer evening leg-stretch to vary a car run—a stroll over Harpenden Common to a delightfully situated inn and then back again, *ad lib*. It can also be connected with Walk 12a.

Use the instructions in Walk 11 to reach the starting place and park. For map see page 44.

The locating point is the Harpenden Arms pub. From here go Londonwards on common land, with the main road to your left, passing the village-type sign and gradually slanting over to the common-side road. Having passed the Silver Cup veer a little more rightwards along West Common.

Just after passing the Rothamsted Laboratory buildings (with the 50th anniversary boulderstone memorial) take the second of two roads on the left, out to the main road and cross over.

This is where those coming from Walk 12a join in. Cross the main road and go down a stony track towards a cricket pavilion. Just before reaching it turn sharp right through a hedge gap and go straight ahead along a grassy track, disregarding a more left-hand one. You subsequently cross a road and pass through bushes, going over more common land. Cross still another road and aim for a point just left of the Golf Club HQ seen ahead.

The path now becomes just rough grass between the smoother greens. Over yet another transverse road the path becomes more marked again, with young trees forming an avenue. Cross yet another road and you come to a cricket pitch with a white boarded pavilion on your right. Go leftwards of this and you will see the charmingly situated Three Horseshoes on your left.

To return to Harpenden take an *ad lib* course over the common. You can't go wrong if you steer a course between the main road on the left and lesser roads to the right.

Walk 13

**Wheathampstead and
Ayot St Lawrence**

5½ miles (9 km)

OS sheet 166

Wheathampstead lies at the intersection of the B651 (from St Albans) and the A6129 (from Stanborough on the M1). There is a car park in the village.

There is the curiously named Tin Pot inn at Gustardwood Common. The sign shows the 'pot' to be a handsome pewter mug with a bacchanalian design. Pewter is, chiefly, an alloy of lead and tin and pewter workers of old often referred to the metal as 'tin'. In Victorian times, a prize cup was often facetiously called a 'pot'. It is quite likely that in former times horse races (or even illegal prize fights) were held on the common and the victor celebrated by filling the prize cup with beer at the little inn. We have noticed a pub called the Silver Cup on Walk 11.

Ayot St Lawrence is famous as the village in which, at the Old Rectory, George Bernard Shaw lived for the last 44 years of his life. You may visit the house at Shaw's Corner.

The 'new' Palladian-style church of Ayot St Lawrence was built in 1778-9 to the orders of Sir Lionel Lyte who started to demolish the old church because—so it is said—it spoilt the view from his house until the Bishop said 'Desist' (or words to that effect).

Just down the lane at Marford you can visit the Devil's Dyke, a Belgic *oppidum*, where in BC 54, Cassivellaunus made his last brave stand against the all conquering Roman invaders.

Before starting the walk I suggest you make a note of the bus service between the Nelson, at Marford, and Wheathampstead, for a short cut back to the start.

At Wheathampstead go along the High Street, passing the Bull on your right and over the river Lea. At the crossroads continue ahead in Lamer Lane. In a couple of hundred yards, and at a footpath signpost, seen ahead, turn in leftwards and go with an iron rail fence on your immediate right.

Over a bar stile continue by a slender path which goes (as I found on my visit) through the crop and so to an iron swing gate to emerge on a golf course.

Here continue with the iron rails on your immediate right and, later, a mellow brick wall to reach a track. Cross this half left and then resume your previous direction, very soon taking a half left

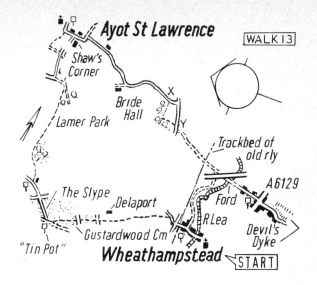

bend. You are now on Gustardwood Common, here given over to golf, so keep an ear open for 'Fore!'.

The clear grassy track takes you through a belt of trees, then to cross a drive. At this point you will see, to the left, a line of cottages which fringe the common.

At the extreme right-hand edge of these is a gleaming white house. Make for a point just short of this and you'll come to the Tin Pot inn. Just before reaching the pub, however, you will cross a road (The Slype). For the ramble point of view turn rightwards in this to cross a transverse road and continue ahead for Kimpton and Shaw's Corner.

Just after passing another attractive inn, the Cross Keys (about 2 miles from the start), and at an angle of brick wall, turn in rightwards on a signposted track, passing nursery sheds.

The track then veers clearly half-left by a path through the crop to reach a woodland corner. Go with the wood on your right. Via an intermediate swing gate you reach, at the wood's end, another stile.

Slant over to another stile, seen a few yards away, and then resume your previous direction along the wooded left-hand edge of a large, cropped, field that was once parkland.

At its end cross a weedy patch by a couple of stiles and continue again by the left-hand side of a field. The path, at first (currently) grassy, soon becomes well defined.

In the field corner turn left over a stile by a gate and follow out the erstwhile drive soon to reach a lane in which turn rightwards. In ¼ mile turn in left on the drive. By subsequently turning right and then left you pass the portico'd front of Ayot St Lawrence 'new' church.

47

After passing through an iron gate with an arch go through a wooden swing gate and, with the wire fence on your left, follow out to a lane angle.

For the ramble route turn rightwards. Disregard a right-hand offshoot at Shaw's Corner. A little later there is a left-hand square bend. Now after just over a mile of lane walking you come to the busy Wheathampstead Road and turn rightwards for ¼ mile to point Y. Turn left here. But, to vary the lane walk (however pleasant) you can, about 100 yards short of the main road (point X), turn in rightwards, with a wood on the right, and in the corner turn square left (subsequently on a thin path through the crop) out to the road at a footpath signpost (point Y). Here take the broad track almost opposite.

Admittedly this open track (a little later take the leftmost of two parallel branches) is rather tatty in places but it soon becomes a pleasant green lane which subsequently crosses the trackbed of a defunct branch-line railway.

In about 250 yards, and by where the Wheathampstead bypass crosses, turn in rightwards on a signposted bridleway. This track later becomes wooded. It remains picturesque, although decidedly muddy and hoof-pounded after a prolonged spell of wet weather, almost to the end when it passes through chemical works to Wheathampstead High Street, where you turn left.

For the Devil's Dyke detour, temporarily disregard the right-hand track just mentioned. Keep on, over the Lea ford (bridged) to the road at the Nelson. Go down the lane opposite to reach, in ¼ mile, the gates (with commemorative plaques) of the Dyke. A public path runs down the centre.

To return to Wheathampstead by footpath, retrace a little of your way and resume the main ramble. Otherwise, I suggest taking the bus from the Nelson. The walking distance is not great but the house-lined road is devoid of interest.

Walk 14

Hertford, Chapmore End and Waterford

7 miles (11 km)

OS sheet 166

No motorist needs telling how to get to Hertford! There is, among other places, a car park at the Warren. But for convenience of description, the walk starts from the main car park adjoining the bus station.

It was in somewhat reminiscent mood that I went over some favourite paths on this route. I recalled, some years ago, how my heart sank when, on the splendid track up to St John's Wood, I found bulldozers at work demolishing the tall hedge on its eastern side. Now, although there must be some loss to flora and fauna, a fine view opens out over the Rib valley which was formerly screened by the hedge.

Whilst realizing generally, that in these days of piped water, many a village pond is now redundant and a stagnant dumping ground of old bicycles and the like, the still-pretty pond at Chapmore End always recalls to me the lines by William Allingham:

> Four ducks on a pond
> A grass bank beyond
> A blue sky of spring
> White clouds on the wing . . .

On leaving the main car park go along Maidenhead Street to the transverse Wash. Here turn rightwards and after crossing the Lea at Mill Bridge, fork rightwards soon to cross the river Beane at Cow Bridge. Then turn rightwards up Port Hill. Very soon turn in rightwards on the Warren drive.

Keep along this elevated way, overlooking Hartham Common and, at its end, continue to St Leonard's Church. Go straight through the churchyard. Pass the church on your left and then turn leftwards out to a lane in which keep forward for Ware Park.

Disregard the first left-hand turn but, after veering rightwards, turn left in Watermill Lane. This is at first residential but is continued forward as a hedged track. Follow it round a left bend and ignore a rightward fork. You then come to another residential section and keep forward to reach a transverse road.

Cross over to a farm road which a little later becomes a very fine track. Continue up to and through a shady wood, seen ahead. On emerging, keep forward more or less parallel to the right-hand

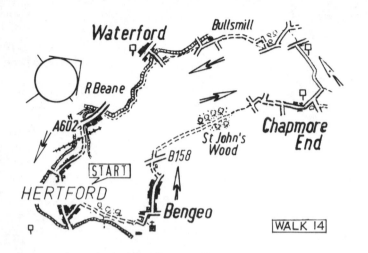

hedge. Cross wooden rails and continue forward with hedgerow timber on your immediate right.

The path now becomes nominally enclosed. You go over a transverse track and again keep forward. At a fork take the right-hand branch. Most of this particular ramble route lies over gravelly subsoil and is reasonably dry after rain. But the stretch you are now in may be muddy after much rain. You soon reach a lane angle however. Keep forward through the hamlet of Chapmore End.

At a T-junction by the pond turn leftwards and follow the road, round bends to Stonyhills. (The name may well derive from the gravel pits hereabouts.) Here is a welcome inn, the Three Harts which, while very isolated, still appears to be viable. Immediately opposite the inn take a footpath (kept open because it leads to the inn?) to a T-junction where turn left.

A lane then comes in from the left. About 250 yards after this, turn rightwards on a track, soon going round a left-hand bend. This, for many years past, has been a 'temporary' diversion of a diagonal path which cuts the corner.

On reaching the farm at Bullsmill, disregard a left-hand lane and also a right-hand one. Only a few yards after this latter, however, take a hedged track slanting off half right with, briefly, the Beane on your right and under the railway. Cross an open field to the cul-de-sac end of a residential road at Waterford.

Go down this and at the T-junction at its end cross over to an iron swing gate. Then follow the riverside path out to the main road in which turn left. In ¼ mile, immediately past a little bridge, turn in leftwards, on a track by a Beane millstream, under the railway, and pass the old waterworks house on your immediate left. Continue forward in Molewood Road. Keep forward in Port Vale. So you rejoin a small part of your outward way and return to the car park.

Note After exceptionally heavy rains it is possible that the Beane may overflow its banks and flood the Waterford meadows. Should you find it thus, just retrace your steps to Waterford and either take a bus back to Hertford (ascertain the times before leaving Hertford) or else walk along the main road until, immediately past a little bridge, you can turn in leftwards and rejoin the main ramble.

Walks 15 a and b

The Ash and the Lea

OS sheet 166

Walk 15a

Stanstead Abbotts, Wareside and Ware

6 miles (10 km)

As the sketch map will show, Walks 15a and 15b can be done separately or combined into a figure-of-eight route, with the node near Wareside. To combine the two, see the note which follows Walk 15b.

For Stanstead Abbotts (Stan Abbotts to the locals) branch eastwards off the A10 on to the A414 before reaching Ware.

There is a car park (at BR charges) outside St Margaret's station (named from Stanstead St Margaret's) and a public car park a little farther up the High Street.

On this walk you will see something of the tiny river Ash (to be met with on other walks in this book) which rises in the Pelhams and joins the old river Lea near Stanstead Abbotts (see map). The Buntingford branch-line railway followed, in its initial stages, the Ash valley and we see its trackbed and go by what was Mardock station. An early '30s timetable in front of me gives five trains a day in each direction. But the last was run in 1964 and despite enthusiastic suggestions the line was not retained as a tourist attraction/old-time railway enthusiast's affair. You will also, on this walk, see something of the Lea Valley Regional Park.

2 miles (3 km) can be saved by using public transport from Ware to Stanstead Abbotts.

From either of the two car parks go up the High Street. Turn left at the top past the photogenic Clock School. About 200 yards past the parish church and opposite Amherst villas turn rightwards on the signposted track which, after passing a few houses, quickly gets you to the wide open spaces.

Continue straight on over a cross-track (point A) with its four-way footpath signpost. After becoming open (a really lovely bit this!), the track becomes enclosed again. You pass a wood on your right. The track then makes a half left bend and soon after this you come to a woodland corner (point B). Turn rightwards (wood on right). You soon reach a pretty house now named Ash Cottage, but 'Doghouse'

52

on the large-scale OS maps! Here go half left to cross, in a few yards, the tiny river Ash by a metal bridge. You will be on clear track. At the field end turn rightwards with the old railway on your left.

Do not cross the bridge then encountered. Instead bear half right. Take (point C) the first left-hand turn. This will take you past the site of the old Mardock station and up the erstwhile approach to a transverse road in which turn rightwards. You very soon take a left-hand turn, past Newhouse Farm. Just after a left-hand branch by the school, turn rightwards on a chine-like path which will bring you out to the Ware road at Wareside, which has two inns, just over 3 miles from the start.

Take the road for Ware, passing the White Horse on your left. In about ⅜ mile (just after passing a right-hand lane which you will recognize as having used on your outward way) turn leftwards on the old Mardock station approach. Retrace a little of your outward way via point C to point B. Here turn rightwards.

You reach the old railway line again with railway cottages adjacent. Cross, and in the field opposite take a course half rightwards of the left-hand trackbed (in the direction of the gabled house seen ahead). The path is usually, in due season, under crop but it is short and brings you to a metal bridge over the river Ash and in a few more yards out to a farm track where turn left with a wall on your left. Skirt (leftwards) the dutch barn seen plainly ahead and go through the stockyard of Watersplace Farm to a transverse farm road in which turn left.

As the stockyard just mentioned may be full of milling cattle (a particular hazard for those with a canine walking companion) one might suggest, presuming on permission, that on reaching the farm track just after crossing the Ash, instead of turning left to the dutch barn as just described, you keep straight on to pass the farmhouse ahead on your right and so out to a farm road in which turn left.

Either way you soon cross the trackbed of the old railway and then the Ash ford (bridged). A little further on (point D) just before reaching the woodland facade ahead, turn rightwards on a clear track, passing wood-fronted cottages on your left. Continue with a wood on your left. Where this wood ends and the track bends left, keep straight on over a park-like meadow to reach a wooded area on the far side. Keep this woodland face on your immediate right and where it ends (where once stood a mellow pump house — now dismantled) keep ahead on a very pretty path with the river on your immediate right. You come to the 'ghost line' again.

Cross this and turn left. At first you have a hedge on your left. At the railway cottage (enthusiasts will note the Great Eastern Railway style of architecture) go right-left to recross (for the last time) the Ash by a footbridge. Over this turn rightwards. Then curve left on a terrace-like path out to a road.

Slant half-rightwards over this and then take a path on the left.

At first you have a hedge (and road beyond) on your immediate right but a little later you make for the stile seen ahead. Continue with a hedge on your left. A clear track then completes your way through allotments on the outskirts of Ware. Here turn left and, in ½ mile, leftwards down Amwell End.

Turn left in Viaduct Road immediately after crossing the Lea (British Waterways Board and the Valley Park authorities prefer Lee). In a couple of hundred yards or so, opposite a right-hand turn, take a footpath, at first enclosed, on the left. You come out on the Lea Navigation, the water on your left. This stretch of waterway (beloved of Cockney anglers) is really a canal which bypasses the much-winding old Lea. You follow the towpath (about 2 miles) to Stanstead Abbotts. (For brief comment on Lea *v* Lee see notes to Walk 19.)

Walk 15 b   Wareside and Helham Green
2½ miles (4 km)

This walk can be combined with 15a for a longer ramble.

For Wareside take the B1004 eastwards out of Ware. Parking is possible just off the main road near the village hall or off the Helham Green road, a quiet one. Or, by arrangement, in the car park of the White Horse. For map see page 55.

On this short round we see more of the old Buntingford branch-line railway including the remains of old stations at Widford and at Mardock. We also see more of the Ash valley.

Go up the lane almost opposite the White Horse at Wareside and very soon take the first right-hand branch. This takes you via Helham Green—note the old pump—down to the B1004 in which you continue leftwards. By a square right-hand bend you cross the old railway cutting by a bridge with the old Widford station to your left. Over the bridge, at once turn squarely right. The path becomes lightly enclosed and you go through a wooden swing gate. Keep straight on, and over the next (wire) fence, enter a large riparian meadow.

Slant half left. You will have the river Ash to your right and will be going parallel to the face of a wood over to your left. For the next ¾ mile or so you will be going along a shallow valley with the river on your right. You leave by a field gate and emerge on a farm road by a little bridge.

Turn rightwards over this and very soon (point C) turn rightwards on a farm road which takes you by the site of Mardock's old station. Continue ahead by the erstwhile approach out to the B1004. Here

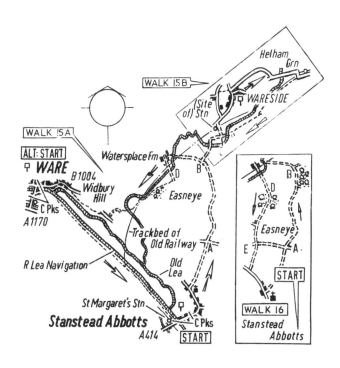

This map covers Walks 15 a & b and Walk 16

turn rightwards. Very soon take a left-hand turn, passing a house which used to be an inn. You also pass Newhouse Farm. Just after passing a left-hand branch, by the school corner, turn in rightwards on a chine-like path. On reaching a lane turn rightwards for a few yards, back to Wareside.

Note To combine Walks 15a and 15b
Follow Walk 15a into Wareside. Here transfer to Walk 15b following the first two paragraphs of that description. For the third paragraph substitute the following:

Turn rightwards over the little bridge and keep straight on, disregarding any rightward offshoots. You will be retracing a little of the outward part of Walk 15a. Follow this, re-passing Doghouse Cottage to a wooded corner (point B) where turn rightwards and continue to Watersplace Farm etc.

Walk 16

Stanstead Abbotts and Easneye

4 miles (6 km)

OS sheet 166

See Walk 15 for instructions on how to get to Stanstead Abbotts and where to park there.

In my ramble route writing I have never, so far, been tempted to emulate supermarket ploys by offering such inducements as (say) 'Fifty Rambles For The Recommended Price Of Thirty'. It is obvious, however, that since many of the rambles in this book can be made into two shorter ones and a good deal of 'perming' done, far more than the nominal number of rambles implied by the title are possible.

The snag is that if too many alternatives are given, the result is often more confusing than helpful. For this reason the present mini-walk, originally a variant of Walk 15a (and sharing its map) is given separately.

In connection with 'walks on wheels' (see notes to Walk 12a) I might add that the Easneye drive from Watersplace to the Stanstead road offers possibilities.

From Stanstead Abbotts follow Walk 15 past point A. At point B continue ahead to Watersplace. On reaching point D, however, *keep straight on the drive*. This goes most charmingly through woods and bracken and later you come (point E) to the head of an avenue, on the left. Here you can either keep ahead to the road and turn left-wards back to 'Stan Abbotts' or turn leftwards down the erstwhile avenue, a victim, unfortunately, of Dutch elm disease, to point A and then retrace a little of your outward way.

Walk 17

Berkhamsted, Frithsden and Coldharbour

7 miles (11 km)

OS sheets 165 and 166

1½ miles can be saved by omitting the Frithsden loop.

Berkhamsted (do not confuse with the Little Berkhamsted of Walk 20) is on the A41 Trunk Road, 28 miles north-west of London.

There is a public car park in the town and another (for which you must pay) outside the railway station.

Berkhamsted Common, partly given over to golf, is a glorious domain which you will enjoy all the more if, especially after a rainy season, you go well shod.

In 1866 Lord Brownlow enclosed four hundred acres of it with an iron fence — torn down overnight by an organized army of protesters. A four-year legal battle followed before the bells of Berkhamsted rang a paean of victory for those seeking 'air and exercise' on this fine open space. From such incidents was founded the Commons and Footpaths Preservation Society.

Either before or after the walk opportunity might be taken to visit Berkhamsted Castle — founded by the Conqueror's brother. It was a royal residence for 400 years and a favourite residence of the Black Prince.

As an easily identified spot, Berkhamsted railway station (though you have come by car and may well have used the other car park) is taken as the starting point.

From the side of the station turn left through the narrow archway and continue with the castle ruins on your right. Ignore the Ashridge turn but just after this as the road (Castle Hill) turns left, continue ahead by the signposted footpath which runs, via stiles, to the metal barns seen clearly ahead. On reaching these turn rightwards in the farm road. Where this bends squarely right keep ahead by a stile on to a woodland track.

In only a few yards turn left on a conspicuous cross-path and follow it uphill through scrub to a transverse wider track. Here turn rightwards to a road in which turn left — still uphill. From the war memorial (point X) soon reached, keep ahead by the signposted track. At an early fork keep rightwards of the signpost.

A few yards before coming out on to a road with posts ahead you will find a bridleway, signposted for Berkhamsted Common, going acutely (V-wise) left. Take this and in about 50 yards turn

rightwards. You will know whether you are at the correct spot because in only a few yards you come to a path enclosed by trim garden hedges.

Scout around if you do not immediately identify this spot. Having turned rightwards as just described, we soon cross a transverse private road and continue by the track opposite. This leads down to the road and to the Alford Arms just under 3 miles from the start. The inn has a garden especially convenient in fine weather for those with children.

With your back to the inn turn rightwards. In about ¼ mile, at a 'deer' sign, turn left on the signposted track. This is a twin brother of the way by which you reached the inn, and equally charming. Thus you go uphill through the trees, over the private road, and by the enclosed footpath out to the common again at a 'Footpath Only' sign. Turn rightwards and at any forks take those which keep you fairly near the golf course on the left.

At 'Bridleway' signs (point Y) you cross a road and continue. In fact as far as Coldharbour Farm your way is always straight ahead, successively over some more open common, through low wooden posts and then cutting a curve of a rough drive. After this the way is, initially, a bit narrower and has many forks. But open farmland will be noted over to the right. Keep parallel to this at first but towards the end you join a corner of it and find yourself on a very clear track, almost a little white road. Follow this to Coldharbour Farm.

Turn leftwards through the yard (the 'Private Property' notice refers to the buildings; you are on a right of way). Through a field gate pass a circular pond on your left and follow the earth track to another field gate. You will now be on a clear farm road, marked by electricity poles.

This subsequently makes a quick left-right turn. Where, a little after, it appears to run into a right-hand field, keep ahead by a stile by a field gate. The path goes with a hedge on the right. In the fenced corner turn left. In only a few yards you come to a field gate.

You now have alternatives. (a) Get over the gate and go half left to Northchurch Farm clearly seen across the meadow. (b) If, like me, you have a dog who may attract the curiosity of heifers, just keep on the track (ie do not get over the gate) to a stile. Turn rightwards over another stile, ie you go around the field and so reach the farm.

At a large greenhouse turn right and then left. Follow the track, with farm buildings on your left, out to the common. Bear a bit leftwards, passing a little over to your left the urn-capped gate pillars.

A little later as the track swings rightwards, housing appears on your left. At a corner of this, at a house named 'Westcroft' turn squarely left on a stony unmade road with housing again left. Where this ends, keep ahead, now with wire mesh fencing on the right. (You are, incidentally, about 550 ft up.) The track is continued to the modernized cluster, with a hedge on the right, but open to the left, of cottages of old Berkhamsted Place.

Pass Warner Road on your right but a few yards past this turn rightwards, downhill on an enclosed path (with fine trees). On reaching a residential road turn left and at the transverse Bridgewater Road, left again.

Then turn right and it's 'This is where we came in'.

Walk 18

**Sandridge and
Childwick Green**

8 miles (13 km)

OS sheet 166

This can be shortened; note possible cuts E-F and/or G-H

Sandridge is on the B651 about halfway between St Albans and Wheathampstead.

One possible car parking space (apparently available to all) is that by the recreation ground. For an alternative start from the car park at Nomansland Common see Note 1 at end.

In addition to the charm of Childwick Green and the pleasantly situated Three Horseshoes on the edge of Harpenden Common there is a splendid track over an upland plateau.

We will take Sandridge church as a starting point easily identified. Turn back in the St Albans direction, keeping on the right-hand side of the road. Quite soon, at a convenient little building turn in, rightwards, on to the recreation ground, keeping by its right-hand edge.

On quitting it, you have two options: either keep ahead with a hedge on your right to a lane, or slant off approximately half left with the electricity line. Both options have intermediate stiles. If taking the first option, turn left on reaching a road and very soon take the right-hand bridleway. The second option will bring you out opposite the bridleway, which we take. The signpost was, I found on my survey, regrettably almost hidden by foliage.

The track (and some of what follows) is no place, after winter rains, for those who come in peep-toe sandals. Do go well shod! The track has, initially, a ploughed field on the right and the farm boundary on the left. It then becomes enclosed. It half-circles Sandridgebury Farm and then strikes off rightwards, at first partly enclosed.

Soon there is open country on the left and the track becomes firmer. You subsequently cross the railway and, in the meadow beyond, veer half right, making for the large green shed.

Pass this on your right, going through the neat farmyard. On soon coming level with the farmhouse, called Cheapside, which lies a little to the left, turn squarely right on a firm drive which later makes a left-hand bend (point C) and finally brings you out to the A6. Here turn right.

In a couple of hundred yards turn in, leftwards, through the

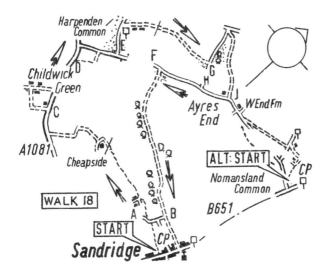

Harpenden Common
Childwick Green
A1081
Cheapside
WALK 18
START
Sandridge
CP
Ayres End
W End Fm
ALT: START
Nomansland Common
B651

ornamental gates of Childwick Bury (see Note 3). Soon bear right-wards and on coming to Childwick (pronounced 'Chillick') Green—a model Estate Village—bear rightwards again and so back to the main road in which turn left.

In ¼ mile you will find (point D), on the right, a short spur of road used as a road-materials depot. Go down (but read what follows) this and from the end take a signposted path slightly left-wards (*not* the track towards the Dutch barn).

At a fence angle you come to, and proceed along, an enclosed path. At its end continue by a green lane, out to the road in which turn rightwards. The green lane just mentioned can be somewhat lush with nettles in high summer, so if your nether limbs are vulnerable you may care to consider the road alternative I have mapped. Either way, immediately before cottages (point E), turn in leftwards on to Harpenden Common.

Keep by the left-hand edge for a short ¼ mile until you are level with the charmingly-situated Three Horseshoes, whose sign will now be in sight.

Take the trackway, passing the inn on your right, and soon going by a bridge over the railway cutting. It is beautiful even if hoof-pounded and soft-going in places. You subsequently come out on a lane (point G) in which you turn leftwards to a junction.

Here you will find a farm track which bisects the angle of two lanes. Turn in on this and follow it out, easily, to a road in which turn right. You pass (and disregard) a lane on the right. A short ½ mile farther on and immediately before coming to a breeze-block barn turn in leftwards (point F) on a roughish signposted track.

This soon, with a hedge on your left, temporarily becomes more footpath-like, but reverts to a track with a long flank of wood (here going by the old Hertfordshire name of 'Spring', Pismire Spring) on your right.

It then veers just a trifle leftwards and, disregarding a cross-track, you pass the end of another wood on your left. It then passes over a plateau-like open field with good all-round views and at another wood ahead touches the 400 ft contour line.

The track has now become a farm road and you keep straight on, disregarding a right-hand turn at point B unless you are doing this walk from Harpenden and do not want to go into Sandridge, finally through a farmyard between sheds and then turning rightwards to emerge exactly opposite the bus stop at Sandridge church.

Note 1   Alternative start from Nomansland Common—a place of much resort on summer weekends with the erstwhile Park Hotel now re-named The Wicked Lady (the sign will explain who she is). There is a large car park in Ferrers Lane, installed in an effort to control the indiscriminate parking which formerly marred this fine common, so named because at one time its ownership was a bone of contention between the rival Abbots of St Albans and Westminster.

Immediately past the car park slant off half right, using any convenient paths and making for a slate roof showing above the trees.

You should arrive at the corner of Lanman Cottage. Pass this and its neighbour on your immediate left. At the transverse green track soon reached, turn left and continue in the rough lane past Amwell Farm to a road.

A snug inn, the Three Oaks, lies a little to the right but for the ramble route turn left. As soon as the open common starts again branch off half right, again picking your own way, so that you reach the road which has been over to your left and continue with it to West End Farm and to point J where the main ramble is joined. On the return, just pick your way, *ad lib*, over the common, rightwards of Ferrers Lane.

Note 2   To be read in connection with notes to Walk 12a. If you are pushing an invalid chair or a kiddie's go-cart note that from the well-house at Childwick Green a drive (a public right of way) extends southwards. If you wish to explore it you can follow this for a mile to a fork, where the half left—now narrower—branch continues the right of way, the half right branch being private. Return the same way.

Note 3   The Childwick Bury drive between the lodge gates and the well-house on the green is not a public right of way but one which pedestrians have been allowed to use in the past. This permission could be withdrawn at any time. If so, just continue in the main road. In ¼ mile or so you pass, and ignore, a little lane on the left and continue for another ¼ mile to point D.

Walk 19

Essendon, the Lea and West End

5 miles (8 km)

OS sheet 166

Essendon can be reached by branching off the A1000 at Brookmans Park. There seems to be adequate space for discreet parking in the village.

Lea or Lee? It is granted that such an ancient name could, in the course of centuries, have established two variants. But 'Lea' seems the most widely used. On Christopher Saxton's map of Hertfordshire of 1577 we find 'Lea fluvius'. Yet in a prospectus issued by the Lee Valley Park authorities we find references to *Lea* Bridge Road. All out of step except our Johnny? Or is there a Mafia-like move among painters of direction signs to create more (even if unnecessary) work? Just one of those things to discuss with the locals over a friendly pint in a village pub!

Essendon is a hill-top village from which there are grand views. Start walking northwards. In a short ¼ mile, take a signposted path which starts immediately past a large house on the right. This leads across a field to a stile in a hedge. A fine path follows (glance back at the church set proudly on a 360 ft high ridge) and takes you to the B158 road in which you turn left.

I note, however, that in one Broxbourne Woods 'Study' (much maligned by ramblers) there was a suggestion that the north-east section of this path be extinguished (possibly in view of future gravel working hereabouts). I hope no such thing happens. But if it *does* (and in a book like this one has to think ahead), note the alternative path (No 2) which strikes off rightwards at former gravel workings and comes out on Bedwell Park Avenue, in which turn left.

This possible diversion, however, is — as it were — in parenthesis. Having turned leftwards on the B158 disregard the right-hand road for Holwell Bridge and at a square left bend turn in rightwards in the waterworks drive.

In only a few yards slant off leftwards on a footpath. After passing through a coppice you go forward on a track with a hedge on the left.

A little later take the left-most of a pair of field gates and go with a line of trees on your right. In the next field the way shifts to have the hedge on your left. Keep on thus, later passing, and disregarding,

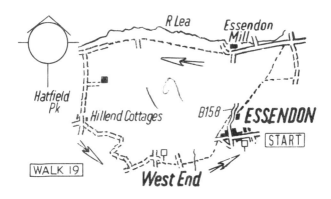

the head of a green lane which comes in on the left. Over to your right is the much winding river Lea.

At the end of the next field go through a field gate on the left and resume your forward way on a roughish track. Where this track joins a metalled road, turn left on an estate road soon passing a farm.

In ½ mile or so you pass Hillend Cottages and still keep on, the road now being rougher as it rises and goes round bends. At a T-junction turn left and then rightwards to the Candlesticks, formerly the Chequers, which has come into view.

From the left-hand side of the inn (as you face it) take a path by a telephone pole to a stile and then through a patch of woodland to another stile. On, now, with a hedge on your left. In about ¼ mile, but before coming to a field corner, get over a stile on the left and follow a slender path through shrubbery. Possibly it will be found to be a bit overgrown, but it is quite short and brings you out to a green lane.

Cross this (the slightest bit leftwards) and take, rightwards, the downhill path, with a hedge on the left. Over a valley cross-track continue by a swing gate and footplanks to a stile and then, without veering left, go up a little bank and continue by the rising path to a wood ahead. Before entering this be sure to turn to admire the very fine view extending over the Hatfield Park woodlands. Go through the wood and a few yards after leaving it go half left over a pathless meadow, aiming for the rightmost of two gaps in the top right-hand corner. Bear a little left, with a hedge on the right, to a stile on the right. By a wicket gate enter the churchyard. Bear rightwards to pass the modern Gothic church on your left. Note the Zeppelin commemorative stone built into an outside wall. So you reach a lane by the side of the Salisbury Crest and turn rightwards, back to Essendon centre.

Walk 20

Little Berkhamsted, Epping Green and Bayford

7 miles (11 km)

OS sheet 166

By using the short lane link B — C the figure-of-eight route can be approximately halved into two separate loops. By omitting the Blackfan Wood section, the walk can be further shortened.

One way to reach Little Berkhamsted (which, within recent years, has streamlined its name from Little Berkhamstead but is not to be confused with the town of Berkhamsted, the starting point of Walk 17) is to take the B158 south-west from Hertford and subsequently branch southwards from it.

Park discreetly at odd places about the village.

The Stratton Tower, or the Berkhamsted Monument, is usually classed as a 'folly'. But Admiral John Stratton, who had the 100 ft tower built in 1789, was no fool. No doubt he had done the Grand Tour of Italy and, following the landed gentry custom of his time, had embellished his estate with an eye-catching tall tower.

As an 'amateur' (in the true sense of the word) of the Sciences he no doubt thought that the tower could be put to practical use, perhaps as an observatory. Building it gave employment to local people and, moreover, second-hand bricks from an adjacent demolished house could be used. The story that the admiral built the tower so that he could view his ships in the Thames is, without doubt, a latter-day grafted-on legend to liven up dull guide books (as in the case of Lady Ann Grimston's tomb in Tewin churchyard visited on Walk 10). The tower, restored in recent years, is in private occupation and is not 'shown'. Those who have been up, however, say (as may be expected) that the Thames cannot be seen from the summit. One wonders, however, whether such a story (of observing ships in the Thames) had its genesis in the telegraph (semaphore) towers mentioned in Walk 4.

From Little Berkhamsted village centre, face the Stores and then go leftwards of it along the right-hand edge of a playing field. Leave by a stile and at once turn left.

The path, with good views rightwards, at first follows the left-hand hedge and then runs through a long coppice.

One soon arrives at an angle of drive. Here keep forward, passing Epping House School. The drive then makes a leftward bend passing a water tower and a radar mast. By the side of the cottage on the right take a path soon through a field gate and then with a garden wall on the right and a paddock on the left. The rough track then becomes hedged and narrow. Look out for a stile on the right. Over this at once turn left and follow the pleasant field-side path, with a hedge on the left, finally through a short enclosed section out to a lane where turn left.

In only 100 yards or so turn rightwards on a tarmac strip by a bungalow named 'Five Acres' to reach a metal field gate. The ensuing path is of an undulating nature and the lower-lying parts where you cross a streamlet can be rather soft after heavy rain.

The path follows the left-hand edge of several fields; in the third it is enclosed. At the end there is, currently, a lightly wired gap, easily crossed, and the path becomes enclosed curving round rightwards to a stony lane. Here turn left.

The way soon becomes residential and brings you to Newgate Street, with its two inns. Proceed in the Cheshunt direction.

In only 100 yards or so turn in leftwards on the Ponsbourne House Hotel drive. There is a pedestrian right of way along this fine, firm, undulating way. Ignore, quite soon, a rightward fork. Past the house the way becomes a farm road and you pass a high garden wall on your left and some silos on the right. Disregard any right-hand offshoots.

You then come to Home Farm Cottage on the left. This is immediately followed by Sankey's Cottage. At the corner of this turn left on a farm track. This, enclosed, runs down to a gate. The way is pot-holed in places but quite clear. It goes through woodland and you suddenly (take care!) come out on a road junction. Here turn rightwards for $\frac{3}{8}$ mile and (point C) take the right-hand turn. Follow the well-wooded road until just after going round a square right bend, you come to a junction (point D). If the weather has been very wet and you are not amphibiously equipped for mud-larking you can turn left, in the Bayford direction, for about $\frac{1}{2}$ mile to point E (see map).

Otherwise keep ahead in White Stubbs Lane (so marked). In $\frac{3}{8}$ mile (just after passing Blackfan Farm on the right and just after woodland starts on the left) turn in leftwards on a signposted track through Blackfan Wood. (*See note at end.*)

You emerge near a small lodge, on a little drive in which you turn left out to a road. Turn left and left again passing the Baker Arms (small car park opposite) on your left. Continue in the Ashendene Road for $\frac{1}{2}$ mile. Then (point E) immediately after passing Bayford House, turn rightwards on a signposted trackway with a mellow garden wall on the right.

Soon veer leftwards, disregarding a forward gate. Continue with a hedge on your right and the Stratton Tower coming into view, curving subsequently a little rightwards to a stone-stepped stile.

Then keep forward, downhill through the wood, over a cross-track to a footbridge. Go half left over the ensuing field to a stile and continue in the same direction to another. Then go with a wood on your left. From an iron field gate the way is continued first as a hedged track and then a drive and you come out on a little lane. On my visit I found local pride in the foregoing path — a new, carved wooden footpath signpost en route, and, currently, white-painted stiles. Turn rightwards for a few yards only and then take a path from a stile by a slatted gate on the left.

So, by the edge of two fields, you return to Little Berkhamsted.

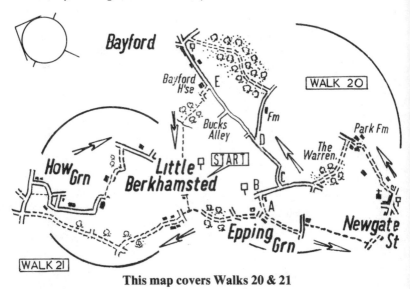

This map covers Walks 20 & 21

Note   When last surveyed, prior to revising these notes, I found that a start had been made (from the northern end of Blackfan Wood) on a pedestrian only path alongside the bridleway. When this is completed, and if the horse-riders keep off it, the pedestrian way will enable walkers to enjoy a ramble through these lovely woodlands without too much mud-larking.

Walk 21

**Little Berkhamsted
and How Green**

4 miles (6 km)

OS sheet 166

See Walk 20 for information on getting to Little Berkhamsted, and parking there. The map for Walk 20 also serves this walk.

As in the previous ramble, face the Stores and then go left of it along the right-hand side of a playing field. Leave by a stile and then turn rightwards to a road. Here turn left and soon take a drive on the right. Follow this lovely way (the pot-holes are easily passable and it's muddy only in a dip) to a lodge at the head of Bedwell Park Avenue, most of the fine trees of which have long since gone.

Go up the broad and rising farm road opposite, bearing right-left round the farm. On joining a lane on the outskirts of Essendon turn left and at the T-junction bear rightwards. At the next fork keep ahead (rightmost fork) and keep ahead again where a lane comes in from the left.

In a short ¼ mile more, and immediately past a large house, turn in rightwards on a signposted path which goes down a meadow and then runs between fields. In ¼ mile from the road you have just quitted, and at old gravel workings, turn rightwards and so reach Bedwell Park Avenue in which you turn left.

In just over 100 yards go through a field gate on the right, veering a trifle leftwards on a rising path, soon to have a garden boundary on your left. So through another field gate to a lane/track in which turn rightwards.

(Note, from my map, an alternative way *via* How Green.)

Having turned rightwards you pass Kennel House. Later, at Ashwell Cottages, turn left. You pass a farm on the right (disregard the private approach). Immediately beyond this turn rightwards along a narrow hedged bridleway and in only a dozen yards turn leftwards through a hedge gap and on to an unploughed baulk. Continue straight over a field. On breasting a slight rise, sheds come in sight. On reaching these continue by a much curving drive out to a road in which turn rightwards.

A little later, turn left in Bucks Alley (so marked). Very soon you come to a stile by a gate on the right. From this take a path by the edge of two fields back to Little Berkhamsted.

Walk 22

Chorleywood, Chenies and Church End

7½ miles (12 km)

OS sheet 166

Chorleywood lies just west of Watford and is reached from Central London via Harrow and Rickmansworth. Branch off from the A404 along, say, Green Street to reach the area around Chorleywood station.

Among possible parking places at Chorleywood there is a small car park in the shopping parade and parking is possible off (but not on) the main common.

The 'escape' from (and re-entry into) latter-day Chorleywood (actually Chorleywood West which has grown up by the station) is remarkably quick and easy. There is the famous common, of course, and there are some fine paths in the council-run Chorleywood House Estate. Instead of being carved up into 'Metroland' woodland building sites, the Whitelands, Carpenters and Hillas Woods are now for public enjoyment and are well managed.

Chenies village, set about the green, is very charming and the church is of much interest. One of the highlights of this ramble is the lovely view over the Chess Valley from near Holy Cross church at Sarratt.

The iron mile post on the A404 just outside Chenies is a relic of the Hatfield-Reading Turnpike. The Cecil family of Hatfield House were fashionable martyrs to gout and were wont to take the cure at Bath. They found their local roads so bad that they decided in the early nineteenth century to develop a short cut (which would also reap a useful income from tolls) from Hatfield to Reading, where the Bath Road was joined. Wags nicknamed this road the 'Gout Track'.

Except for one spot, duly noted, I did not find any specially wet spots. I have often wondered, however, why a walking-stick is usually regarded as an encumbrance or as a sign of senility. It is useful, even in midwinter, for slicing at a trailing bramble. But, to the point, it is extremely helpful as an aid to balance when circumnavigating large puddles.

As an easily identified location, we will take the line of shops called New Parade near the railway station as the starting point. Keep straight on, in Whitelands Avenue, and just after passing Carpenters Wood Drive on the left, turn in on a signposted footpath. Do not take the first right-hand path (the one which runs along the

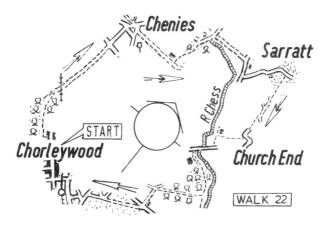

immediate backs of houses) but turn right on the next one a few yards further on. It runs, clearly enough, at first half right and then with your back to the houses, to reach a transverse path along which turn rightwards, just inside the edge of the wood.

Go over a prominent hoof-beaten cross-track and continue until you soon reach another edge of the wood. Here turn rightwards and follow a meandering path just inside the edge of the wood. You come to that prominent track again and turn left in it (probably alongside it), again just inside the edge of the wood. It goes under the railway.

Do not be dismayed if you find the next few yards of enclosed track decidedly wet after prolonged rain.

As the lane rises it becomes, mostly, almost arid by comparison. On coming out on the main (A404) road turn left (disregarding the lane opposite) for about 100 yds. Then at the iron mile post turn squarely rightwards along a signposted hedged cart track. Soon, turn rightwards on a similar track, from which you get a good view of the Manor House with its twisted Tudor chimneys.

On coming out to a lane bend, keep forward but then curve clockwise (ie disregard forks to the left). So you pass the Bedford Arms at Chenies and, a little later, come to the Red Lion. Turn leftwards through its car park. In the open field reached turn left and, very soon, rightwards across the field (with the telephone line). You thus reach an estate road and turn rightwards to the farm seen ahead.

On reaching the farm, pass through the side of the farmyard and out through a gateway. Almost immediately turn left over a stile in a hedge. You pass a dutch barn and its surround.

71

Continue by the field edge and in the corner turn rightwards to reach a pair of stiles on the left. So you enter Mount Wood. Follow the path, later with a post and wire fence on the right. The path runs downhill and the river Chess appears ahead. The path runs out to a track which might be regarded as a green lane. Turn left in this, over a pair of stiles and so out to a lane in which turn rightwards.

At a fork bear right, with the watercress beds on your right, to cottages seen ahead. At the road angle there, turn squarely right. At the next fork turn leftwards uphill, for you are now down in Sarratt Bottom. Disregard the signposted path soon seen on the right. Continue (noting the rearward views), until just after passing a newish house on the right, you come to the wooded Dawes Common. Here slant off half left and take the leftmost path after a few yards. When you reach an unmistakable cross-track, turn rightwards. Cross the lane and continue by the signposted path from a stile opposite.

Keep generally forward but when the white rectory is seen through the trees, slant half right towards it to an iron swing gate and along by the path between a beech hedge and bracken. The path runs out on a drive. Keep forward but soon take a path from an iron swing gate on the right. The path has a wood on its left for a few yards but then keeps forward, by an open path along a slight embankment. The roof of Holy Cross church then comes in view. Pass its porch on your left. Make for a stile (footpath signpost) just to the right of the almshouses.

The path, with a fence (initially of Goldingtons) on your right, runs down to the valley. Here turn leftwards and so to a road in which turn right. Immediately over the bridge turn leftwards on the waterworks drive. By stiles clearly seen ahead keep forward to and into a wood. Just as you are about to emerge from this at an iron swing gate, turn rightwards over the adjacent wooden stile (I found, on my visit, both the swing gate and the wooden stile in a tatty condition) and go uphill, just inside the wood. You later find yourself on a pleasant drive. Just after another track slants in from the left, turn left on a prominent road-like drive and so out to the main road.

Cross over and veer a trifle rightwards on a wide grassy sward between trees. On reaching the road keep forward. A short distance past the Rose and Crown turn rightwards down Colley Land (which is the name of the lane).

On reaching a transverse road turn right for a few yards then go left, under the railway and then rightwards, back to New Parade in Chorleywood.

Walk 23

**Bricket Wood and
Aldenham**

3½ or 7 miles (5.5 or 11 km)

OS sheet 166

Bricket Wood and Aldenham lie, respectively, north-east and east of
Watford. For convenience of description, Bricket Wood station car
park is taken as the starting point. It can be reached by branching
off from the A404 just after its intersection with the M1. Or you can
branch off the A5 near Colney Street. If you decide to base the walk
on Aldenham, this village is also reached from the A404 or the A5.

Parking is possible in the yard of Bricket Wood station though this
is an unmanned halt. There is parking space around the common at
Smug Oak, too.

It is only from the map that, generally, you realize how near you
are to Watford, the largest town in Hertfordshire. At one point you
will see the tower blocks of Watford on the skyline — but only if you
look backwards! Apart from the Green Belt, Bricket Wood Common
has so far served as a buffer to Watford's expansion in this direction.
Drop Lane ford and Munden House ford are really delightful,
especially on a warm day.

From Bricket Wood station turn left and very soon go rightwards
down Drop Lane, passing the Ambassador College entrance. At its
foot, at a pretty ford where the road turns squarely left, turn rightwards over a stile (which is often masked by a parked car).

You will have the little river Ver on your left and soon come to the
actual spot where it joins the river Colne. A little beyond this,
cross by the bridge and continue by the path to join a bridleway on
the far side. Turn rightwards in this. Soon disregard a right-hand
track to a farm. Just after entering woodland, however, note a
right-hand drive by a lodge (point X).

If you are doing only the short option you turn rightwards here
subsequently to join point Z (see Note at end). But even if you are
doing the full round, make a brief detour here as it is one of the
highlights of this ramble. You soon come to a very pretty ford over
the Colne. The full round turns *leftwards* at point X. Thus if you
are returning from the ford you cross the bridleway and keep forward
on the narrow, rising bridleway, subsequently past the tree-screened
works.

At a transverse track turn right. At square left bend keep straight
ahead, through farmyard with cartsheds, at first, on your immediate

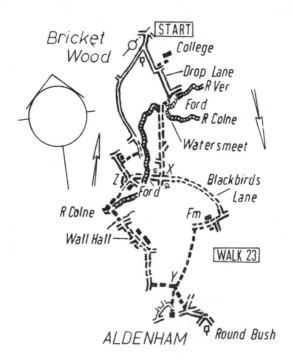

Bricket Wood

START

College

Drop Lane

R Ver

Ford

R Colne

Watersmeet

X

Z

Ford

Blackbirds Lane

R Colne

Fm

Wall Hall

WALK 23

Y

ALDENHAM   Round Bush

left. Continue in the forward farm road. Soon take a left-hand track. This is followed with a hedge, and at one point a wood, on your immediate left to where (point Y) a path—an unploughed strip very obvious in winter but where, in summer, its grass may tend to merge in with adjacent crops and so require looking for—strikes squarely right.

If you do not wish to go into Aldenham (immediately ahead and where the church has showed up proudly from a distance) then turn rightwards here.

Otherwise (for Aldenham) continue by the left-hand hedge. The path is rough but passable. Just before cottages ahead slant leftwards up a slope and, so, forward in the rough lane, to Red Lion Cottages. Enter the churchyard by the lychgate opposite. At once fork left. At the corner of a wall turn left. Follow out Church Alley to the new road. Go forward a little way, cross and then take a path on the left, adjacent to the Edge Grove drive. Cross the playing field diagonally, making for a stile that appears to be to the left of a pylon prominently ahead (go leftwards round the field edge if school games are in progress). Take the clear path to a further stile. Here, at point Y, continue ahead over the open field to a drive. Turn right.

Subsequently veer half left (for Otterspool), passing the college buildings. Where the main drive turns left, keep ahead. Go over a transverse track. Keep forward to go, in a few yards, over a dried-up former watercourse. The erstwhile bridge here is almost completely collapsed but, fortunately for our present purpose, not apparently needed now. Walk on to the metal bridge and over this bear half right. No marked path shows but on breasting a rise you will see a drive over to the left.

You gradually slant over to join this at a wooden post (seen ahead). Turn right and bear left at the fork. Very soon, at another wooden post (one trusts that these wooden posts — privately erected footpath signs — survive the ravages of time), bear half left aiming for a point just to the left of a red roof ahead. On reaching a drive turn leftwards. Immediately after passing through a field gate, with a cattle grid alongside, take the adjacent stile on the right. In the meadow strike a course midway between the left-hand hedge and the forward electricity line to arrive at a clump of bushes screening a tiny pond, behind which is a stile. Continue by a line of trees, passing an old orchard on right, to a bar stile.

Go forward to a wire fence then left-right round it down to a farm road at cattle sheds. Turn left in the farm road. On coming to a lane turn right and follow it round to Bricket Wood.

Note Link X — Z. Over the ford, the drive passes Munden House (on the left) and over a cross-drive curves gently rightwards soon passing point Z.

Walk 24

**Rickmansworth and
Moor Park**

8 miles (13 km)

OS sheet 166

Rickmansworth is easily reached, being at the intersection of the
A404 and the A412. You can park opposite Rickmansworth station.

At one point on this round you meet (and can photograph, if you
have brought flash equipment as it's in a shady position) an iron
Coal Post. A tax was once levied on all coal coming into the Metropolis and over a century ago a ring of iron posts was set up to indi-
cate the limits of the Corporation of London's jurisdiction in the
matter.

With your back to Rickmansworth station, turn right and soon
go right under the railway bridge to the High Street. Turn left
but soon swing right in the bollarded-off Bury Street. Follow this
round a left bend and then turn right in the transverse Church
Street.

Go through the churchyard to cut off a road corner. Then cross
over ignoring new roads on the right, and subsequently cross the
bridge.

Curve left in Moor Lane (the A4145). Ignore new roads on the
right. Opposite Rickmansworth Lodge take a drive signposted for the
golf courses. In only a few yards and as indicated by a footpath
signpost, climb over a stile on the right. Regard the drive as a
flexed bow and your path as the bowstring. Keep just left of a
rougher grass area. You'll soon be back on the drive again by the
bungalow-like public clubhouse. Starting from the side of the
professional's shop you will see a conspicuous uphill track.

The mile-long path you now walk (Public Footpath 54) used to be
marked by a series of short white posts but these have now gone. A
compass is not essential but if you have one take it along. The
direction is south-east throughout. Just follow my directions, keep an
eye cocked for 'Fore' and enjoy the feel of fine turf underfoot and
the scenery all around.

So go up the track by the professional's shop. When the track
ends keep forward but right of the near bunker. Shift a little to the
right and then go forward on a clear path. Follow this out into the
open, with the grey bulk of Moor Park mansion seen ahead, and
proceed with a woodland flank on your left. On reaching a lime
tree which stands out a little turn half right. Then make your way,
following, as best possible, the line of the invisible path over greens

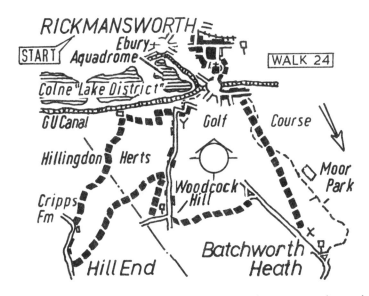

and round bunkers, and the like. No one in my experience is likely to bawl you out if you are considerate of others' amenities. When you reach the main drive again you will be about ¼ mile short of Moor Park mansion.

Continue half right across the drive; do not go less than half right. If you soon find that you have a scrub and woodland flank on your right and are being forced down to the drive you are *not* on the right track! Your aim is to get to the far right-hand corner of the golf course. Your final landfall (not seen yet) is a large house with conspicuous white gables. Preceding this (on your right) are a few large houses, a long red brick wall and some iron railings.

By the right-hand side of the white gabled house you will find an enclosed path which is followed out to a private road in which you turn right and then right again (point X) in the Batchworth Heath Hill Road.

In case of difficulty just find your way back to the main drive and keep on it, presuming permission, past the mansion, which is open to the public on certain days. Then you go round a large right-hand curve, and out to Batchworth Heath Hill Road where you turn right, past the pub to point X where you keep straight on.

After about ½ mile on the main road and immediately past some new housing on the right, turn in left on a road spur at Primrose Lodge and almost at once fork left on a downhill hedged track. At the bottom of this get over a stile on the right and at once turn left resuming your former way, to another stile which is now in view.

Keep by the left-hand hedge looking carefully for a stile (easily missed as it lies behind a tree) with a white arrow waymark on it. Cross the meadow half left of your previous direction to pick up a wood on the left. Keep by this, ignoring a left-hand gap. At a transverse hedge go through a gap which once had a stile. Only the concrete step-supports remain but there is a footpath signpost here.

Cross the next meadow half right to a stile (in view) and follow out the enclosed path. I found it quite passable—I hope it is regularly trimmed. It brings you out on a lane but be careful if you have kids or canines racing ahead.

Turn left to the photogenic Rose and Crown (about 3½ miles from the start at Rickmansworth) and by the inn turn right in the Harefield Road. In 300 yards, at the Hillingdon sign, turn right through a bits-and-pieces apology of a wooden swing gate. Cross the meadow diagonally to a stile in the far corner, just left of an open shed. Maintain the same direction to cut a corner of the next field to a bar stile. This may have to be looked for but it is perfectly negotiable. Don't try to force a way elsewhere.

Then maintain the same direction over a field to where a farm road meets a public road. There are footpath signposts here. Do not, however, enter the road but slant back along the gravel-bed farm road. At the entrance to Fieldways (currently a riding establishment) keep straight on, with a hedge on the right, to a bar stile and on again beside what looks like a cut-down hedge to, and over, foot-planks which span a little stream. There is a footpath signpost here. Then uphill, hedge on right, through various erstwhile hedge gaps now mostly fenced and provided with stiles, and with footpath signposts at intervals. Finally you go out to the head of a short residential road at Hill End.

Go down this and then turn right in the transverse Springwell Lane. In about ¼ mile, as the lane bends left, take a signposted path from a good stile by the side of a decorative white gate. Go forward by the side of a farmyard and continue along a gently descending hedged track for 100 yards or so. Then, as directed by the footpath signpost, turn right on a track with, at first, a wire fence on the right and then a wood.

Just before reaching the field corner you will find a footpath signpost. Here turn left and slant over towards the right-hand woodland. A little way along this you will find a stile with a crooked arrow painted on it. This means that you get over the stile, turn left for two or three yards, turn right over another stile and at once left. But immediately you have got over the first stile just mentioned, note, on the right, the iron Coal Post. It has either never been set in the ground at all or has been shifted and not again set in.

Go along the bottom of the sloping field, with a ditch on the left, to a corner. Then turn right uphill where you soon meet a gravelly farm road along which you turn left through a gate. In theory, after passing through this you should shift a little to the right before going

78

forward again parallel to the farm road.

The farm ahead is Stockers, where the *Black Beauty* TV series was filmed some years ago.

Make for the right-hand end of the farm buildings to join a farm road in which you turn right. Immediately before the large water-works building turn left over a stile. Cross the meadow half left of your former direction. Then straighten out. The path, soon enclosed, runs out to a road (point Y). Here turn left.

Follow round a right bend followed by a half left one. Where the road bends again, turn left in Frogmore Lane. You soon reach a bridge over which you turn right down to the canal and then left with water on the right.

Just before reaching the Batchworth bridge again, and if you have sufficient daylight time in hand, note a little bridge on the left. Over this you can follow, quite pleasantly, a path through the Aquadrome grounds to the Ebury roundabout subway and so back to Rickmansworth station.

Walk 25

Braughing and Patmore
Heath

8 miles (13 km)

OS sheets 166 and 167

Approach Braughing northwards from London via the A10 which is on the line of the Roman Ermine Street. At the north end of the Puckeridge bypass take the B1368 to Braughing.

Entering Braughing, turn rightwards down Malting Lane. Cross the ford and bear left past the Methodist chapel to the Axe and Compasses. You can park in the square opposite the pub.

This is a walk in what has been called the Puckeridge Hunt Country, completely rural and not much visited, except by such connoisseurs of country walking as yourself. I found on my survey that for most of the way walking conditions were quite good. Yet followers must not expect well-trodden paths at *all* points. But there are no real difficulties. The walk is, however, best done other than in high summer conditions (when crops may be high).

Braughing (pronounced 'Braffing'), our base, is a delightful and compact little village with many picturesque corners to attract your camera. It stands on the tiny 'never-heard-of-it-before' river Quin, a tributary of the Rib.

About 50 yards beyond the Axe and Compasses take a narrow path between houses on the right. This soon goes along the left-hand side of a playing field and allotments and emerges on a road by cottages.

Turn rightwards and in just over 50 yards take a footpath on the left signposted for Patmore Heath (2¼ miles distant). Very soon cross a stile to an open field, seemingly a permanent sheep pasture.

Bear slightly left making for a gap in the hedge at the far end where is a stile. Cross a second field to a farm (with radio mast) ahead. This field could be ploughed but I am informed that the paths are regularly trodden by local 'vigilantes'. May they continue their good work!

Continue in the road past the farm. In a short ½ mile you will see a white gate on the right. Continue in the road for about 200 yards beyond this gate to a point where the road enters the grounds of a large house called Cockhampstead. Here turn rightwards off the road and go along the edge of the field. The true path which runs across the middle of the field has been ploughed out but the detour I describe is obviously acceptable and used by horse-riders. You pass the Cockhampstead garden on your left. The moat can be

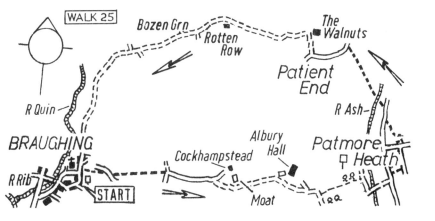

glimpsed through the trees.

A little beyond the moat go through a gap in the hedge on your left. The path now goes straight along field edges with a hedge first on your left and then on your right. It brings you to a group of estate cottages by a pond, a real picture-postcard scene!

Turn rightwards in the estate road (you are in the Albury Hall domain) for ¼ mile. A drive with double gates marked 'No Footpath' comes in acutely on your left. Continue for just under a hundred yards and then go through a small gate on your left. Turn rightwards along the field edge with a wood on your right. The white cottages of Patmore Heath, your next objective, can be seen ahead a little to the left.

At the field end go through a gate and continue along another field edge with, now, a wood on your left. At the end of this turn rightwards on a crossing track. This soon turns left through a field to cross the stripling river Ash which rises in the Pelhams not far north. Your way then runs between hedges, left of a farmyard and out to a road.

Turn left and in a few yards take a path signposted for Patmore Heath. Where this path joins a road turn left alongside Patmore Heath. This is a genuine heath albeit a minuscule one: a nature reserve, in fact.

You soon come to a T-junction and turn left, down to the Old Catherine Wheel which is about 4 miles from the start. Turn rightwards in the main road. Take, in about ¼ mile from the inn, a footpath on the left signposted for Furneaux (pronounced 'Furnix') Pelham. It is the *second* left-hand path you come to; disregard one on the right.

The path may be ploughed for a short distance but the way ahead is clear. Make for the footbridge with the white handrail.

After crossing the footbridge go ahead on a fine grassy path, which I am glad to say I found unploughed, between fields.

Where this path joins a lane, note the picturesque thatched cottages on the right. Our way is, however, to the *left*. In ¼ mile you come to a post box labelled Patient End. Here turn rightwards along a track. Immediately after passing a large house called The Walnuts the track swings left across fields to pass a group of trees on your left (although I notice that the OS map shows the track skirting the trees on your right).

Soon after this, look for three trees by a ditch on your right. On reaching this point do *not* take what seems the 'obvious' route straight across the field to a broad bridge. *Instead*, turn rightwards and go along the field edge with the ditch on your right. In the corner of this field I found the remains of a gate which, no doubt, marked where the path once went.

Now here comes one of those not at all unusual 'practical' diversions from the theoretical official definitive path which makes sense from the farmer's point of view and which causes no inconvenience to the rambler—provided, of course, the unilateral diversion is recognized as such and is not a subtle opening move in phasing out the right of way.

So, in the corner of the field just mentioned, do not go through the old gate but, instead, turn left. Cross the ditch on your right at any convenient point and continue for a few yards with the ditch on your left to the corner of a field. Here turn rightwards and proceed with a deep drainage channel on your left. Cross a concrete footbridge and continue with the channel on your right to a pond where bear rightwards to a house named Rotten Row.

A 'made' road goes off to the right but our path keeps straight ahead along a field edge with a hedge on the left. At the left-hand corner of this field look for an intriguing 'secret' track. Go, without difficulty, through trees and scrub for about 20 yards to a broken-down field gate.

Pass through this. There is a short stretch of barbed wire on your left. Then bear rightwards. The track runs through a narrow belt of trees. From now on, simply follow this track without digressing to left or to right.

After a while it becomes broader and then, after passing a sign to Bozen Green Farm, becomes a grassy path. After passing a house named Bozen Green the track is very overgrown for a short distance and you will find it easier to presume on permission and walk carefully and considerately along the edge of the field.

But then, as inevitably happens, you have your reward. You join a clear sunken track which emerges into open fields and leads you pleasantly into Braughing. Where the track joins the road continue ahead and in a few hundred yards you are back again at your parked car.

Walk 26

Much Hadham and Barwick Ford

8 or 5½ miles (12 or 9 km)

OS sheets 166 and 167

To reach Much Hadham from London take the A10 and 3 miles before Hertford branch rightwards on the A414 (for Stanstead Abbotts). At the end of this village turn left on the B180 and so through Hunsdon and Widford into Much Hadham. Park discreetly in the village.

This is a truly rural part of Hertfordshire. For most of the way the going is good, and whilst there are no real difficulties for moderately experienced country walkers there are one or two places (these are mentioned in the description which follows) where, for quite short distances, the rambler must be prepared to strike out for him or herself. This is obviously much easier at such times of the year when crops are not high.

We find two fords (see my map) over the Rib and there is, for some, the interest of the course of the old Buntingford branch-line railway.

The shorter option is obtained by using the X-Y-Z link. See note at end. A mini-walk of about 2½ miles could be obtained by starting from Barwick Ford and, at point Y, continuing to point X and so via Biggin's Farm.

Taking the Bull as starting point, walk north (ie away from London) for a couple of hundred yards. On the left-hand side of the road by a lamp post and nearly opposite Hall Cottage take a footpath between a cottage on the left and a high brick wall on the right. This path leads gently uphill between trees and becomes a broader track.

Just beyond a right-hand bend in the track you will see a clear track leading through a farm gate on the left. Ignore this! As so often happens, the 'obvious' track is not the correct one to take; continue by the grassy track.

Shortly afterwards a gravel track comes in on your left. Here go forward through a wooden field gate (not the iron one). Continue with a hedge on your right to the end of the field. Here go through another gate and continue along the side of a field, this time with a hedge on your left.

At the end of this field go through a small gate in the hedge. Then keep ahead to the left-hand corner of a wood. Follow the edge of this wood for a short distance and at a concrete hut — presumably a relic

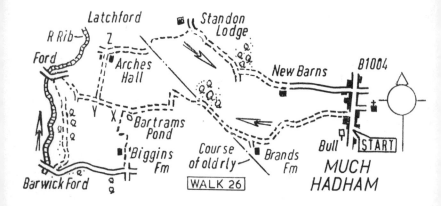

Map labels: R Rib, Latchford, Standon Lodge, Ford, Arches Hall, New Barns, B1004, Z, Y X, Bartrams Pond, Biggins Fm, Course of old rly, Brands Fm, Bull, START, Barwick Ford, WALK 26, MUCH HADHAM

of the old Buntingford branch-line railway which will doubtless be of interest to some readers—go half left across the field to a line of prominent oak trees. On my visit I found this last section ploughed but not difficult to follow.

Now go forward on a clear track, but shortly after passing the last oak tree turn squarely left on a path with a hedge on the right. Where the hedge ends, turn right.

In about ¼ mile you will come to a clump of trees and bushes surrounding a small pond (usually dried up in high summer). This is point X.

Now be careful! For the full round do not take the 'obvious' track on the left alongside the pond; it is a false trail. Keep to the main track and go a few yards beyond the pond. Then turn left and make your way across the open field.

From here to Biggin's Farm the foregoing path doesn't exist on the ground at all, but there is no problem in finding the line of it. On my visit I found the field grassy but it is possible, on the crops rotation principle, that it might be ploughed. I found on my survey that the stile at Biggin's Farm is in fair condition, a reassuring sign. So—make for some tall trees at the end of a thin hedge about 200 yards away. On reaching these go forward with an open ditch on your right to a field corner. Here turn left for about 100 yards and then go through any convenient gap in the hedge on your right stepping without difficulty over or through the wire. This wire is clearly not intended to obstruct walkers. It is probably to keep cattle from wandering. Then go alongside a field with a hedge on your right to a stile at Biggin's Farm.

If, as described in the preceding paragraph, you fail to find any convenient gap in the hedge, just go with the hedge on your left towards Biggin's Farm. As long as you can follow the main direction, do nothing to damage fences.

At Biggin's Farm continue forward on the farm road to cross-roads and here turn rightwards for Dane End (one of, I think, four places in Hertfordshire so named).

After a pleasant ¾ mile and by a 'Ford' sign (Barwick Ford being just ahead) turn rightwards on a bridlepath signposted for Latchford. This goes uphill through a beech wood and then along the left-hand edge of a field. Where the track swings right, look out for a small path on the left (easily missed!). After a few yards this goes alongside a fence on the left.

Continue with woods on your right and the river Rib glimpsed between trees on the left — a beautiful stretch, this!

After about a mile, pass through a field gate to a meadow beside the Rib and, following a line of trees across the meadow, emerge to a lane in which turn rightwards. After 100 yards turn rightwards on a footpath signposted for Much Hadham. The path soon emerges in a field. The path now runs uphill in a depression on the left-hand side. At the top you join a farm track at a right angle (point Y). Here turn left following the track across fields to Arches Hall, plainly seen ahead.

At Arches Hall turn rightwards on a footpath signposted for Much Hadham. Two miles away this goes, at first, between hedges and then along a field edge with a hedge on the right. Subsequently across the trackbed of the old railway to emerge on a large field. This may be in plough but the way ahead is obvious ... simply make for the large double gates in the hedge on the opposite side of the field.

Through these cross another field going to the right of the farm-yard, not through it. Through a gate you come out on a bridleway. Here turn rightwards on a broad track and keep on it until you reach New Barns. The barns are much in evidence but they 'ain't so young as they used to be'.

Forward, now, along a lane for ½ mile to Much Hadham where turn rightwards for the Bull.

Shorter route At the pond (point X) continue in the track you have previously been following for another ¼ mile and then turn right-wards (point Y) following the track across open field to Arches Hall (point Z).

Walk 27

Much Hadham, Wareside and the Ash

9 miles (14.5 km)

OS sheet 167

To reach Much Hadham from London take the A10 and 3 miles before Hertford branch rightwards on the A414 (for Stanstead Abbotts). At the end of this village turn left on the B180 and so through Hunsdon and Widford into Much Hadham, where you can park discreetly.

For a start at Widford church (see also Walk 10) just turn leftwards, in Widford village, on the B1004. The church, with its prominent 'Hertfordshire Spike' spire, is soon reached. You can park just short of the church in one of the two lay-bys, which are marked by official parking signs.

This is Charles Lamb's country. At the close of the eighteenth century a certain Mary Field was housekeeper at Blakesware near Widford. Here, at holiday times, she invited her grandchildren — one of whom, Charles Lamb, was later to achieve fame under his pen-name of 'Elia', as a genial essayist.

In these writings he recalled in, for example, *Dream Children* and *Blakesmoor in H ... shire,* those happy days of his childhood, disguising, as just seen, the name slightly.

He also liked a tipple in the Bell at Widford. It was his 'local' in fact. With only a slight detour we can visit the inn on this walk and can see, there, a plaque commemorating this association with Lamb. Mary Field is buried in Widford churchyard — with her name spelled as Feild.

It was Lamb who originated the famous tag 'Hearty, homely, loving Hertfordshire'. He could never resist a pun. Incidentally, Herts is usually pronounced 'hearts', though Hertford is often 'Harf'd'.

As this is a circular walk, it can, alternatively, be started from Widford church (½ mile from the village). A possible advantage is that in 3 miles you reach the inns at Much Hadham. (There are no other inns until you reach Wareside.)

From Much Hadham, turn Londonwards. By the side of the war memorial turn in rightwards on a drive. In about 200 yards, look out for a stile on the left.

From this go half left of your previous direction aiming, over the meadowland, for the left-hand end of a group of farm buildings

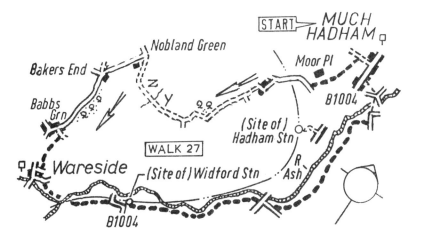

seen ahead. Several stiles mark the way.

After passing a little rightwards of the large new barn make for the white fencing, with sloping tops, ahead and, over a cattle grid, reach a lane.

Turn right, and ignoring minor offshoots, keep on, over the old Buntingford branch-line railway (a nostalgic sight!). On approaching Kettle Green ahead fork left. At the farm turn right and, very soon, left.

Then keep ahead disregarding a right-hand offshoot, and, later, a left-hand one. A magnificent open track takes you over a field to a wood. Through a neck of this, by a field gate, continue with the wood on your right bending rightwards with it. Then take a square left-hand turn. Now be careful!

Where this earth track ends and becomes a farm road in 200 yards or so turn squarely right. You get the impression you are on a grudgingly retained rough field-side path with a hedge on your right. Actually you are on a bridleway that has got overgrown. But if you persevere you will find that the rough places are counter-balanced by easier ones and ⅜ mile after a left-right bend at the field end you emerge on a clear, much hoof-marked, track. Here turn rightwards.

This track soon curves rightwards and a little later you come to a left-right-left kink, here crossing a deep-set stream by a little bridge (point Y). The track soon bends rightwards (point Z) and is followed out to a lane elbow at Nobland Green. Technically the couple of hundred yards between points Y and Z must be regarded as permissive, but I saw no minatory notices on this quiet way.

It is likely that your eye has been caught by the clear track

87

running rightwards. If you follow this (it is a public right of way) you will come, in 250 yards, to a tiny bridge on the left (point Z). If you cross this, turn left and then right and you will come, at the next right-hand bend, to point Y previously mentioned and follow out to the lane elbow at Nobland Green.

At the lane elbow turn acutely left passing, in ½ mile, through Bakers End and then, in another ½ mile, to Babbs Green.

Just before reaching a telephone box turn in left on an enclosed path. Just after crossing a concrete footbridge turn right (at an iron post) steeply uphill, twisting to a stile.

Then follow the right-hand hedge of a field finally over a minor road and by the side of the village hall into Wareside. Turn left in the road.

Very soon, by a little pumping station, turn rightwards. Do *not* cross footbridge but turn left with a small tributary stream, which is likely to be dry in summer, of the Ash on the right. Follow to a stile and a sturdy metal footbridge after which turn left, following the river Ash to and over old railway track. Then turn left, with a hedge on the left, to a road.

Here keep straight on, past old Widford station to the church which is conspicuous ahead. Widford village lies about ½ mile ahead but for the ramble route enter the churchyard and pass left of the church to a stile where you will enjoy a good view. The path to take is clearly seen—down, right then left, parallel to a tree-crowned embankment.

At the field end take an enclosed path through a small swing gate by the Ash. On leaving it slant over the meadow to a farm road. Cross and go along the waterworks road. Pass the building on your right (now by a path). Keep by the left-hand hedge and trees, with the Ash over to the left, out to a road. Slant half left across it. Turn right in the Perry Green Road.

Soon, at a lodge, slant half left, through a gate just to the right of a barrier. You are in what, I presume, is a Herts CC road grit depot. Pass a weighbridge platform on your right. Then veer a little left across a circular arena. The hedged bridleway you now take is seen ahead.

Follow it out mostly with a wood on your right. It narrows in places but is perfectly passable—and very lovely!

When later, with wire on your immediate left, you find the path becoming overgrown and crowded in, just shift slightly to the right. You'll find a good track which ultimately brings you out to a lane in which turn left. Where this bends right keep ahead by the forward footpath which brings you to a pretty ford.

Cross by the left-hand bridge. Turn right and, in a few yards, turn in left on an enclosed path which brings you out by an old-fashioned school-house to the main road. Here turn rightwards, back to your starting point.

Walk 28   Widford

6 miles (9.5 km)

OS sheet 167

To reach Widford church from Hertford and Ware continue by the
B1004 through Wareside. Just short of Widford church park in one
of the two lay-bys, marked by official parking signs.

This is another ramble for Elians since, like the previous walk
(to which I refer you) it is in Charles Lamb ('Elia') country. Also of
interest are the tiny river Ash and the course of the now-defunct
Buntingford branch-line railway which closed down in 1964 after
a hundred years of existence. Now that the 'permanent way' is
anything but and with much of the old trackbed being ploughed up
and incorporated into neighbouring fields (though some has been
converted into farm roads) these old railways attract considerable
interest.

From the lay-by make for the church. On reaching the village name-
board turn rightwards, as indicated by a public footpath sign,
through gates and proceed down a field with a wire fence on your
immediate left.

At the far end turn leftwards through one gate then rightwards
through another, thus continuing your previous direction along the
track beyond. At a junction continue forward soon crossing an open
field. The rough track then becomes hedged again, eventually
bending half left towards a farm called Filletts.

On reaching this, take a right-hand branch—a track which passes
between farmhouse and outbuildings. It veers leftwards and you
come to another junction in which you turn rightwards. On coming
to a field, bear rightwards with the track. You should, technically,
now slant off half left to reach the far field boundary at a corner.
If, however, the field is in crop, just keep along the track to the end
of the field and then turn left for 100 yards.

Either way, go through a hunting gate and then bear rightwards
round a little pond to reach a hedge along which turn leftwards
with the hedge on your right. I found on my survey that recent
ploughing had somewhat 'shaved' the track but the passage of horse-
riders had sufficiently re-made it.

You soon have a wood on your right. Go round a quick right-left
bend and then, a little later, a left-right one. The ditch you pass at
this point is an ancient homestead moat. Such moats are

89

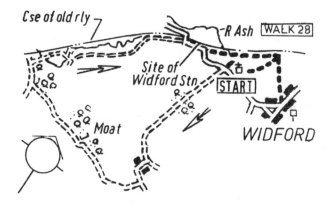

comparatively common though in many cases the wooden buildings they once surrounded have perished. These homely moats had no military significance though they did keep out roaming thieves and vagabonds at night, as well as rampaging herds of wild deer, swine and the like. They served for drainage (and sewage one has to admit) and could be used as fish ponds, an essential source of food supply in former times.

At the field end continue ahead along a grassy track to reach a more prominent transverse one. Here turn rightwards. In 300 yards, at the corner of a wood, you come to a junction. Here turn rightwards, with the wood on your right, down to a pretty little white house most appropriately named 'Ash Cottage' now, but which was until fairly recently 'Doghouse', a name still retained on the large-scale OS maps. One wonders whether this was just a typical example of rustic humour or if it originated from the fact that a hunt retainer in charge of hounds once lived here.

Do not go left with the track in front of the cottage. Instead, continue ahead by an enclosed path between power poles, soon crossing the little river Ash by a metal footbridge and continuing by the track beyond to a transverse one. Here turn rightwards having, in a cutting on your left, the old trackbed of the 'ghost' Buntingford branch-line railway.

Do not cross leftwards the bridge now reached. Instead, turn *half rightwards* along the track into the valley. Disregard, soon, a left-hand offshoot but just after this, immediately you have re-crossed the Ash, turn leftwards through a gate into a narrow meadow.

Walk the whole length of this meadow and then pass through a gate to enter another. This meadow widens and you keep along it with the Ash for company a little to the left. You subsequently enter

90

another meadow and continue, half left of your previous direction and parallel to a wood over to your right. You then closely approach the river and come to the old railway trackbed. Do not cross this. Instead, turn rightwards alongside it, up a slope and then down to an enclosed section of the path, still alongside the old line.

In due course you come out to a road by a bridge. Cross the road and continue ahead, using the adjacent sidewalk, soon passing the site of old Widford station on your left.

Where the road bends squarely to the right, turn in left, through gates on to a signposted bridleway which runs along the edge of a meadow, with the old railway trackbed on your left. By a broad bridge you cross the meandering Ash.

Continue to the end of the meadow. Here cross a stile and then slant half-right to the river-bank. Turn left along this to a footbridge which you cross and then resume your way by the riverside to a stile which gives on to an enclosed track. The footpath opposite leads up to the village of Widford and those who are in search of refreshment may well take this path, returning to their parked car by road (see map).

For a direct return to Widford church, however, turn rightwards in the track just mentioned. It soon brings you to a meadow. Head for the conspicuous church. On reaching the bank below it climb up to a stile at the left-hand end of the red-brick farm boundary wall. By this stile you enter the churchyard. And so you reach the road in which turn rightwards, back to your starting point.

Walk 29   Ware and Wadesmill

7 miles (11 km)

OS sheet 166

Ware is on the A10. It has several car parks. The most convenient for this present walk is in Broadmeads, just off Amwell End, immediately over the railway level-crossing.

Ware, an old malting town on the Lea, still retains much of its old-world charm. Some parts (as, for example, West Street along which we pass at the end of the walk) haven't changed much since Frederick Griggs was sketching here for the still much-loved *Highways and Byways in Hertfordshire* (1902). There remain many little courtyards (seek them out!) which, although now often occupied by trendy folk, still look as if they expect to hear the rattle and creak of harness and the grating of iron-tyred coach wheels on the cobbles.

But buildings get old and past economic repair (for example, in Crib Street at the beginning of this walk). Not all can be preserved though it is a great pity that nothing seems to be done (I should be glad to learn otherwise) about the once lovely gazebos, or summer-houses, which flank the Lea, and which we will see at the very beginning of this walk.

On this walk you will pass Thundridge old church, abandoned in 1853 when a new church was built on the main road about five furlongs to the west. We will pass this 'new' church a little later in the present walk. Only the creeper-clad west tower of the old church remains.

Although Ware itself has a fantastic number of inns (until recently there were three adjacent in a row in West Street) there are no others on this ramble route except (towards the end) at Wadesmill.

Go up Amwell End and soon, at the bridge, turn left along by the Lea. Cross by the first metal footbridge and go through a car park out to the High Street. St Mary's church is in view. Pass this on your right, going past the war memorial and along Church Street.

At Cusick House turn left into Crib Street and, ignoring side turnings, follow to a transverse road called The Bourne. Here go left.

Immediately after passing the Canon Tavern, with its martial sign, turn rightwards in Milton Lane and in a matter of a few yards, opposite Thundercourt, turn rightwards down a narrow alley-way which in a few yards bends squarely left and runs, enclosed, at

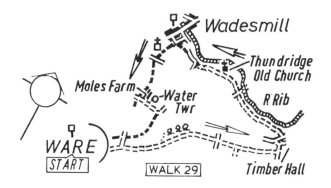

Wadesmill

Thundridge
Old Church

Moles Farm

o-Water
Twr

R'Rib

WARE
START

WALK 29

Timber Hall

the backs of gardens.

Through guard rails it emerges on a green strip — a recreation ground — where you keep always forward with a stream over to the right, to emerge through more guard rails on a road named Kings Way.

Here turn right and, very soon, left in High Oak Road. In 250 yards or so, ignoring roads on the right, you come to a footpath signpost — currently vandalized, I'm afraid — on the left.

Slant off here, passing the bungalow/lodge on your left, disregarding, soon, a conspicuous left-hand offshoot. Keep straight on. You have, on your right, wire mesh fencing enclosing what might appear to be a covered reservoir but which is, I think, the banked-up end of a playing field.

Open farmland follows and you have a ditch and stream on your left. Keep always forward. The track, now open and going slightly uphill, passes a grand oak on the right and brings you to a woodland facade, seen ahead.

Keep this always on your immediate left. At the end, where it recedes to the left, keep straight on over an open field passing another sentinel-looking oak on your left. You subsequently pass through a hedge gap and under the farm electricity line and again continue unerringly ahead. The track is now a little narrower but quite clear.

Over a transverse track the way broadens out into a farm road and on soon reaching the next field picks up a hedge and tree-lined ditch on its left. A view of the Rib valley opens out on the left and cottages at Cold Christmas hamlet are seen.

On reaching a transverse farm road turn left and in front of Timber Hall bear left out to an angle of lane. Here turn rightwards. In a couple of hundred yards turn left in a little lane signposted as a public bridleway. It runs downhill and comes out into the open where you continue forward and then, on reaching the river Rib, turn left. The pleasant riverside track is followed up to and over a transverse drive. Here you continue ahead although the river now recedes out of sight to the right. Before long you come to Thundridge old church.

Having looked around continue in the farm road out to a lane elbow. Here keep forward but in 100 yards or so slant off half-left on a quite prominent open path up to a bar stile. For a few yards you have a fence on your right and then continue across the field (a paddock) to another stile.

The path which follows is enclosed and narrow but it seems always to be kept fairly well trimmed and soon brings you out, suddenly, through a white wooden swing gate to the Windmill.

At once turn left on the enclosed path signposted for Ware. This rises, making use of steps, and goes past the 'new' church of St Mary. It comes out on a short residential road called Woodlands, which is followed forward to a transverse one.

Cross over to take a signposted, track-like path opposite, passing an electricity transformer on your immediate left. An electricity line shows the way and our objective, the water tower of Moles Farm, is seen. By a stile you enter another field and have a deep ditch over to your right.

On coming, just before a woodland patch ahead, to a field gate on the right, go through and follow the open, grassy track which ends at a stile, to the farm ahead. Go by the farm road passing farm buildings on the left. Just before reaching a wooden swing gate immediately ahead, turn left by the farmhouse and, proceeding by short square bends through farm buildings, pass between the water tower on your left and a pond on the right. Then follow the clear farm road for a short ¼ mile to where it bends left.

At this point turn squarely right. There was once an open track to follow but on my visit I found it footpath-like with sheep wire on the left. It is followed easily enough, later picking up a hedge and ditch on the left and it finally brings you to a cross-track/path at an angle of concrete fencing posts.

Turn left, but very soon look out for and get over a stile on the right. The path enclosed by wire on the left, and a hedge and ditch on the right brings you, over a stile, to a drive.

Keep forward, very soon over a prominent cross-drive and by a facing stile on to a forward path. As it is enclosed you just cannot go astray.

On reaching housing the path bends squarely left and then right. On coming out to a road you will recognize point X on your outward route. Retrace a little of your outward way through the green strip of recreation ground. For variety, however, on reaching the far end of Crib Street continue ahead through the churchyard by a short avenue, passing the church on your right.

On coming out to a transverse road do not continue at once to the High Street but bear left in West Street. So, veering finally into the High Street, we finally turn rightwards in Amwell End, over the Lea and back to the starting point.

Walk 30   Broxbourne and Bencroft Woods

5 miles (8 km)

OS sheet 166

This is really a two (or even three) in one ramble route. The basic walk as detailed goes through Broxbourne Wood and later you skirt Bencroft Wood. Apart from any *ad lib* roaming in the latter you will find two waymarked routes either of which, or even both, can be included with the basic Broxbourne Wood ramble or left for a future visit. Having discovered the delights of these delectable woodlands (two of several in what is broadly known as the Broxbourne Woods area) you will want to return. And incidentally the lanes in this district form a fine 'scenic drive' for motorists.

This is one of those walks best done in summer when the warm sun has had a chance to dry out the land and when one appreciates the cool shade of the woodlands.

Both Broxbourne and Bencroft Woods are owned by the Hertfordshire County Council. There are considerable differences between them—contrasts which you will enjoy. Broxbourne Wood was in commercial production when the HCC took it over and the policy continues.

But do not imagine that you will be walking on straight paths through serried ranks of dark conifers. The 'rides' and paths vary a lot in width and there is much deciduous matter. One path— possibly the highlight of this walk—winds most alluringly through almost virgin woodland.

I have, in Broxbourne Wood, kept mostly to pedestrian-only ways. These are railed off with squeezer gaps to allow a walker's entry but not the horse-rider's. There are plenty of other tracks open to equestrians.

Bencroft Wood, however, is at the moment practically all 'ancient' woodland, though one part is currently being coppiced.

There is a considerable tangle of lanes in this area and since motoring visitors may be coming from various directions the best plan might be to give Bayford railway station as a locating point. This remarkably lonely station is one station short of Hertford North. From Bayford station go left up the hill to Brickendon Green. Just before you reach the Farmer's Boy take the right-hand turning, for Wormley.

Now cruise along quite slowly so as not to miss two landmarks. In ⅝ mile from Brickendon Green look out (point A) for a hedged

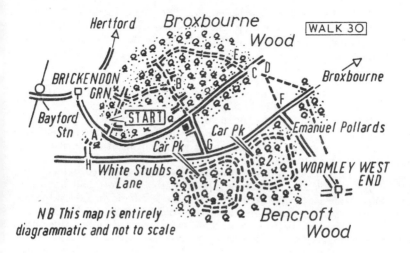

Hertford
Broxbourne Wood
BRICKENDON GRN
Broxbourne
Bayford Stn
START
Car Pk
Car Pk
Emanuel Pollards
White Stubbs Lane
WORMLEY WEST END
NB This map is entirely diagrammatic and not to scale
Bencroft Wood

bridleway on the right. It is signposted for White Stubbs Lane. I suggest that you make a preliminary investigation, say for about 50 yards, along it. If (and this will only be after a spell of dry weather) you find it walkable, you can, as described later, return along this bridleway. But if it is too muddy and hoof-mauled, don't worry, I will suggest an alternate.

After this preliminary exploration, return to the car and continue in the road for another couple of hundred yards. You will then see (be careful not to miss it) a clear dead-straight farm road running off left. The farm road is open on its left and is headed by a modest Broxbourne Woods sign. Just inside here, as indicated by another sign, you may park your car (free).

Continue up the clear semi-'made' track. Just *before* coming to a dip turn in rightwards through rails on Path No 6 (so numbered by the wood's conservators). The entry is not seen until you are abreast of it but it is directly opposite another branch on the left.

The 'path' is, in fact, a wide, grassy ride which goes down to a dip and rises to give exit, through rails, on to a narrower track.

Here (point B) turn left. Soon ignore a railed-off branch on the right but continue down to a dip (you are on a horse-riders' track and it can be muddy in this hollow though one can normally skirt round it easily enough).

At the top of the rise you meet a transverse way and turn right-wards on a walkers' path. This is a most delightful way, very narrow and much winding but quite clear since it is maintained by the HCC. It is almost impossible to go wrong as there is only one way through the thick wood and the path is waymarked No 4 at frequent intervals.

Keep a keen eye on these waymarks. There comes a point however, when according to the map, the No 4 path makes a very sharp V bend rightwards. I found it very difficult (point F on my map) to detect the turn-off point for this sharp V branch and, in fact, it is not followed on this route. You will note that the waymarking changes to No 5 and this is the way (forward) we take. It brings you out to a lane at a stile and notice board (point C). Cross to the signposted stile practically opposite.

If by chance you *did* happen to follow the V branch of No 4 and come out on a cross-track with a stile and the lane just to the left, don't worry in the least. Just make your exit and then turn left in the leafy lane to point C.

Over the stile (opposite point C) go to the next (in view). My impression is that the correct line of path now goes half left to a fairly wide cattle gap halfway along the left-hand hedge and then continues in the same direction to a stile (point D) in the far left-hand corner of the next field. This way is perfectly followable. But if you make for the left-hand far corner of the first field, ie ignoring the hedge gap, you will find a stile and over this go along the hedge to point D.

Over the stile at point D you have two options. (a) If the field is not in crop (I found it in grass) go half left over it—in single file please—looking out, as you get near it, for a stile ahead. This gives on to a lane in which turn rightwards.

Alternatively (b), from point D go left a few yards and then squarely rightwards on a grassy track out to a lane where turn rightwards.

Either way ignore (point E) the left-hand lane unless you wish to detour to the Woodman (in which case see Note 1). Keep straight on in White Stubbs Lane to come to the entrance car park of Bencroft Woods on the left.

For convenience of description (but see Note 2) ignore the entries (there are two car parks) to Bencroft Wood on the left. Keep on until you reach a right-hand turn (point F). You have a choice of ways here. If the preliminary inspection of the bridleway mentioned at the beginning of this walk indicates that it is usable, then ignore the right-hand turn and continue in White Stubbs Lane and after ½ mile or so you will come to the southern end of the required bridleway on your right (point H). Take this. It runs at first with a long woodland strip on your right. It then veers half right to reach a transverse lane at a point (A) which you'll recognize as 'this is where we came in' and you turn rightwards to the car park.

If, however, the preliminary inspection of the bridleway indicates that it would be too wet for comfort, just go up the lane at point G.

Follow it out, to a transverse lane. Here you can turn left and follow out to your car parking point. But better: at the lane junction re-enter Broxbourne Wood by the very coy main entrance and immediately veer right at the fork, passing the map board on your immediate left. You will be on a straight bit of dark-surfaced woodland track and soon come to point B again. Here retrace a little of your outward way—with different views and lighting—back to your starting point.

Note 1 At point E you can, as already indicated (and a signboard points the way) proceed to the Woodman at Wormley West End, about ¾ mile along the lane. To vary the return to rejoin the basic route, take the signposted path opposite the inn. After a few yards it becomes enclosed, and may be a bit overgrown. But you soon reach an open field and continue uphill, with wire on your left, to a stile. There is a nice rearward view of the inn in the valley. Over the stile slant slightly rightwards and go along the right-hand edge of a beautiful wooded common called Emanuel Pollards (so spelt on OS maps). One wishes that a certain type of visitor had tidier picnic habits. You reach a lane and turn left in it, repassing the left-hand lane (point E) and keeping straight on.

Note 2 Unless you are very pressed for time, you will surely give Bencroft Wood at least a brief look-in and possibly reserve a more detailed exploration for a further visit. Note that there are two car parks. From each of these a circular waymarked trail goes. Look carefully for the marks on the trees.

Bencroft Wood doesn't seem large enough to get seriously lost in. Except at one point, which is signposted, where an exit can be made by a public footpath, the wood is surrounded by a fence. Those with normal good hearing might, if attentive, hear cars passing on White Stubbs Lane.

Note that the westernmost car park is west of point G so that if you are emerging from this western car park, you turn *rightwards* to reach point G or *leftwards* to reach point H.